FREED

to be ME

Published in 2009 by
New Life Publishing, Luton,
Bedfordshire LU4 9HG

British Library Cataloguing in Publication Data
A catalogue record for this book is available
from the British Library

ISBN   978 1 903623 38 1

Typesetting by New Life Publishing, Luton

FREED
to be ME

Margaret Duncan

published by
New Life Publishing, Luton

CONTENTS

For my children
Simon, Sara, Helen, Mike, and Tony
- I hope you learn from my mistakes!

Also in memory of two good men,
David and Warren,
whom God endowed with
endless love and patience!

The Mission of My Life

God has created me to do Him some definite service.
He has committed some work to me,
which He has not committed to another.
I have my mission - I may never know it in this life,
but I shall be told it in the next.
I am a link in a chain,
a bond of connection between persons.
He has not created me for nothing.
I shall do good. I shall do His work.
I shall be an angel of peace,
a preacher of truth in my own place,
while not intending it,
if I do but keep His commandments
and serve Him in my calling.
Therefore I will trust Him,
whatever, wherever I am.
I cannot be thrown away.
If I am in sickness, my sickness may serve Him;
in perplexity, my perplexity my serve Him.
If I am in sorrow, my sorrow may serve Him.
He does nothing in vain. He knows what He is about.
He may make me feel desolate, make my spirits sink,
hide my future from me - still He knows what He is about.

John Henry Cardinal Newman

INTRODUCTION

For most of my life I have worn a 'mask'. It started in childhood when feelings of rejection developed into a deep seated sense of inferiority, ending in self-loathing. I felt unloved and unlovable; I was a nuisance; a pest and a burden and I carried these feelings into adulthood.

Over the years the masks changed according to my surroundings, but the reasons for wearing them remained the same. But masks don't really protect you - they're sweaty and uncomfortable and they don't really fit. They even prevent you from seeing yourself as you really are, so that eventually you lose all sense of self and become a chameleon, eager to please others at any cost and despising yourself more and more for doing so.

Having been raised a Catholic, I never read the bible. I didn't know that I was 'fearfully and wonderfully made' or that God had 'put me together in my mother's womb'

(Psalm 139). I thought I was just an unwanted 'accident'. I had never heard that God loved me 'with an everlasting love' (Jeremiah 31: 3) or that even if my mother forgot me, God would not, because He had carved my name on the palm of His hand! (Isaiah 49: 15-16). Even if I had read these words I would never have applied them to myself. No, God must mean somebody else, everybody else, but not me.

When the masks no longer worked, I began to drink to numb the pain and eventually drink-fuelled self-loathing led me to the brink of suicide. In desperation I cried out to the God I wasn't even sure really existed; and if He did, I was sure He wouldn't like me either. But God didn't give up on me and He sent Jesus into the darkness that surrounded me, releasing me from the prison of self-hatred. Jesus said: "I have come to give sight to the blind and set the captives free..." (Luke 4: 18-19). I was spiritually blind and although my prison had no bars, it held me captive and prey to the lies of the enemy. Jesus led me into the light, smashed the last of my masks and set me free to be me.

Oh, give thanks to the Lord, for He is good! For His mercy endures forever. Psalm 136: 1

CHAPTER ONE

Seeds of Rebellion

Before I formed you in the womb
I knew you
(Jeremiah.1: 5)

"I'll never forget you! I promise I'll never forget you!" I shouted as the car disappeared from view at the top of the long and winding drive. Frantically scribbling down the registration number on a scrap of paper, I vowed that one day I would trace the owners of the car which was speeding off with my most precious possession. Anger welled up in me as I punched the wall in frustration. I wept bitter tears and swore that nobody would ever hurt me again. How had I ever got into such a mess? Little more than a year ago I was still at school with a bright future ahead of me but right now I had never felt more miserable in my whole life and at that moment I felt I had nothing left to live for. In the year since I had left school I had grown up quickly and life had taught me a bitter lesson.

It was January 1965 just after New Year, a time when people make resolutions, a time of new beginnings and the promise of a fresh start. I had just turned eighteen, an age when I had my whole life ahead of me but I felt as though I had the cares of the world on my shoulders and right then I just wanted to die. Strangers had taken away my beautiful little baby and I would never see her again. How had it all gone so horribly wrong?

I was a 'late baby', the youngest of seven children. Mum was 42 years old, Dad was in ill health and unemployed and yet another child was the last thing they needed. I was born on the 15th of October 1946 in Barrow-in-Furness, a ship-building town in the North West of England, and should have been named Teresa after the great saint on whose feast day I arrived. However, this was my grandmother's name and my mother didn't get on with her. My mother was an easy going person but unfortunately my grandmother was a bigoted Catholic from the north of Ireland who never accepted the fact the Dad had married a Protestant. No way was my mother going to call this latest addition to the family by the same name as the woman who caused her so much strife in her marriage and so she named me Margaret! From the moment I arrived on the scene there was trouble.

As I was growing up I loved to watch the great ships taking shape as I walked past the dockyards and I remember when the cruise liner 'Oriana' was built. Always a dreamer, as I looked at the beautiful sun deck I fantasised about the glamorous people destined to sail on her. I had a vivid imagination due to the number of books I read and the weekly visits to the cinema and I pictured myself strolling the decks dressed in the latest fashions, drink in one hand and cigarette in the other as I gazed into the sunset. I was a lonely child, frequently locked into an imaginary world where I was rich and famous. As I had a gift for imitating accents, I often amused myself by pretending that I was American and took great delight in spinning yarns when-ever I had an audience. America fascinated me from an early age and it was one of my childhood dreams to see the skyscrapers of Manhattan and the Great Plains of the West and the Rocky Mountains. It was all a far cry from the little council house that was home, but my day-dreaming provided a much needed escape route at times.

My early years were happy. As Dad was unable to work due to ill health, we were very close and he took me out most days to the local park.

"Be careful you'll fall," shouted Dad as I hovered over the park lake eagerly trying to catch minnows in a home made net. We had a lot of fun and I wasn't aware that we were a poor family, although obviously my parents had a hard time making ends meet. I took it for granted that everybody had old army and navy greatcoats on their beds to keep them warm at night! My parents, like many others, had learned to survive the 'Great Depression' when millions of men and women were unemployed and it was difficult for even young, strong men to find jobs. Somebody as frail as Dad had no chance. It was a humiliating process standing in line each day outside the factories hoping that somebody would give you a few hours work and some who couldn't face the shame of unemployment committed suicide, creating even more heartache and hardship for their families.

People talk about the 'good old days' but few of the unemployed who survived the Thirties considered them anything but times of grinding poverty and ill health. The infant mortality rate was high and those who survived were often sickly. My older brothers and sisters suffered from rickets, a disease caused by lack of calcium and general malnutrition, unheard of today except in developing nations. Another embarrassing scourge which was common then was ringworm which attacked the scalp. Sufferers had to have their heads shaved and painted with gentian violet which marked them out for all to see. The only consolation was that there were so many of them they were unremarkable!

Dad, although officially classed as an unskilled worker, was actually highly skilled and could turn his hand to almost anything around the home. It was he who made the curtains for our house, using the old treadle sewing machine. He would also make coats for the boys if he could get hold of a discarded overcoat. Dad loved to visit the local salerooms where he could pick up an old bike or some furniture to repair and restore and sell on for a few shillings. One of my favourite outings was a trip to the local gasworks where Dad and I filled a wheelbarrow with coke. Dad would push me through the streets in a homemade wheelbarrow consisting of a large wooden orange box attached to old pram wheels. Once we reached the gasworks it was a scramble to fill the barrow with as much coke as we could. Coke was much cheaper than coal and didn't give off as much heat but it was all we could afford.

I thought it was great fun, running around the busy yard dodging the coal trucks but in fact it was dangerous and more than one child was killed dodging between the coal wagons in the hope of picking up the odd piece of 'real coal'.

Another place I loved to visit was 'Cobbler Bill's.' Bill was the wizened old man who repaired our shoes and his tiny shop was actually the front room of his little terraced house. I loved to stand on the rickety chair peering over the high counter as Bill hammered and shaped the leather. "One of these days Bill you're going to swallow those nails!" his wife joked as he filled his mouth with nails and rapidly spat them into his hand before hammering them into an assortment of shoes. The modern 'while you wait' repair shops can't compete with Bill's tiny shop with its wonderful smell of leather and the sound of machines buffing and grinding away.

In those pre-supermarket days the local Co-op was another shop filled with wonderful smells of tea and coffee, cheese and hams. There were very few pre-packed goods around then and basics such as tea and sugar were weighed on the spot. A special 'cheque number' was issued to each member of the Co-op, and dividends were paid out annually according to how much had been spent so it was very important to quote this number after every transaction. When Mum sent me on an errand to the Co-op I ran down the road chanting the number over and over like a mantra. It was important not to forget to give it to the shop assistant as Mum used her annual dividend to buy me a new outfit at Easter. This was an exciting day for me as we visited various shops in the town in an effort to get something which was both smart and cheap. One Easter I remember particularly well as my mother took me to a second hand shop where she bought me a little skirt and matching jacket. They were much too big for me so we had to go along to another little shop where a lady did alterations. I was so proud when we went to collect my suit and mum bought me a little hat to go with it and I walked proudly to church that Easter Sunday in my new outfit. I had a new pair of shoes too which I was only to wear on Sundays or going into town with my mother. The rest of the time I wore little black canvas shoes which soon wore out as I was quite a tomboy and it wasn't long before my toes would be peeking through the worn canvas.

Biscuits were a luxury in our house and if I was lucky I was sent to the shop to buy half a pound of broken ones. I suspect that more than once the kindly shop assistants 'accidentally' broke a few to fill my little brown bag. People also bought damaged fruit which was sold off cheaply, especially late on Saturday afternoons and we thought ourselves lucky indeed to get a few apples and pears, even though they were a bit bruised; a far cry from the stringent EC regulations of today!

Dad was Catholic, and one of my earliest memories is of being taken to Mass each Sunday, where I would sit on his shoulders at the back of the church. For some reason a lot of the men stood at the back of the church in those days and made a dive for the door as soon as Mass ended. I later learned that most of them made for the nearest pub which was pretty typical of Catholics in those days in complete contrast to our Protestant neighbours who walked solemnly to church in their Sunday best and behaved with the utmost decorum. They frowned on drink and looked down their noses at these common Irish Catholics who couldn't get out of church fast enough and into the nearest pub, only returning home at closing time, often the worse for wear. As Mass was in Latin it was very exotic and the bells and clouds of incense rising into the air added to the drama of it all. I was enchanted by the whole scene and enjoyed our weekly visits to Mass which would be followed by a delicious Sunday lunch. Although we were poor my mother was a very good cook and made a little go a long way. Home-made soups, casseroles and pies were our weekly fare and on a Sunday, Mum made a delicious roast dinner followed by rice pudding. Sunday was the one day when we got a pudding so it was something to look forward to. On Monday Mum used the leftover meat to make Cottage Pie or Shepherd's Pie as we called it.

All in all life was good and the first cloud on my horizon was when my favourite cousin fell to his death whilst climbing in the Lake District. Jimmy, on holiday from the seminary where he was studying for the priesthood, was an experienced climber but one mistake cost him his life. I couldn't understand why I would never see Jimmy again or ride on his broad shoulders and although I didn't know it then, this was a forerunner of the heartbreak ahead. Jimmy was the only son of my Dad's brother, Uncle Jim and his wife Aunty Marion and although they had two daughters whom they loved dearly, they never really recovered from this terrible loss. Uncle Jim was a lot of fun and I used to love going to his house with Dad. They would sit around the table drinking beer and telling funny stories. Dad was not much of a drinker due to his ulcers, but Uncle Jim like the rest of their family enjoyed a good drink. I remember pestering my Dad to let me have a taste of his beer, threatening to tell Mum he'd been drinking if he didn't! And so at the age of four I blackmailed my Dad into giving me my first alcoholic drink, which I must admit I didn't really enjoy. However this was the beginning of a fascination for alcohol which would have devastating consequences in the future.

The other shadow looming in the autumn of 1951 was the knowledge that I was to start school after Christmas and the very idea terrified me. I celebrated my fifth birthday in October and my parents tried to prepare me for school, telling me how much I would enjoy learning many new things. Apparently I was a child who was forever asking questions and my parents thought that school would be good for me but I had a sinking feeling in the pit of my stomach at the very thought of it and my fears proved to be well founded. Dad did his best to reassure me, promising to take me to school each day and collect me as soon as the last bell rang. "Don't worry love" he said as he ruffled my hair "we'll still have plenty of time for our outings after school's finished." But still I couldn't shake off the feelings of terror and the awful sense of dread made me physically sick.

Dad had been ill for years; he had duodenal ulcers and would go quietly off to his room at times when he was in great pain. He always made light of this and disliked any fuss preferring to suffer in silence. At the end of October he suddenly became very ill and was whisked off to hospital; I never saw him again. The surgeons did an exploratory operation revealing an advanced cancer of the stomach which explained the terrible pain he'd suffered for so long. Until the very end Dad had hidden his own suffering in order to console others. We still have a letter written by the other patients on his ward telling of Dad's gift of laughter to his fellow sufferers. Apparently he would look out for anybody who was very fearful or depressed and do his best to cheer them up and speak words of hope to them. My beloved Dad died on the 3rd November 1951 and my happy little world was never the same again. Before I even started school I had experienced the pain of bereavement twice and I believe this planted seeds of insecurity which would bear bitter fruits in the years ahead.

The sudden disappearance of this person who was the centre of my little world was devastating. The worst thing was that every time I asked where Dad was, people quickly changed the subject. I couldn't understand what I had done wrong for him to have left me like that and like many children who lose a parent, I blamed myself. Had I been a bad girl? Such thoughts plagued me but every time I asked when Dad was coming back I was told that he had 'gone to be with God.' Well I didn't want him to be with God, I wanted him to be with me, so whoever this God was, I didn't much like him already! Obviously the family thought they were acting in my best interests but it was a terrible mistake. To make matters worse, Dad's coffin lay in an upstairs room until the funeral. I remember people trooping past me up the stairs to the bedroom where the 'big box' was and my peering through the banisters, desperate to glimpse what was in there. On the day of the funeral somebody must have taken care of me, but I have no recollection of this. I do remember constantly searching the house and garden looking for Dad and running to the window when I heard the garden gate opening. I knew one thing - he had loved me dearly and would never have left me. If only somebody had tried to explain to me what had happened to him. I was to put this experience to good use in later years.

The next few weeks were spent in a haze of misery and confusion. Even Christmas had lost its sparkle and only brought the dreaded school closer. The day finally dawned when I had to leave the house clutching my sister Sheila's hand and tearfully waving goodbye to my mother. Because Dad was a Catholic all the children had been brought up in the faith and this caused a lot of friction between my parents. When Dad died my mother had apparently toyed with the idea of sending me to the local State school rather than the Catholic one. However, she felt it would have been unfair on me and to her credit she made sure I always went to Mass each Sunday, once I was old enough to go alone.

Religion had been the cause of rows between Mum and Dad, made worse by the interference of my grandmother who was dogmatic and prejudiced against Protestants. To make things worse, a priest had insulted my mother, telling her that she would go to Hell because she was not a member of the 'one true faith.' This was a very harsh judgement on a poor woman who was trying her best to raise a large family in trying circumstances. To be fair to Mum, she did her best to instill good moral values and principles in her children and often quoted from the bible, something which was alien to Catholics in those days as very few, if any, even owned a copy of the bible. My mother was suspicious of all things Catholic and would never have set foot in a Catholic Church or school and her attitude didn't help me any as I made my way in this alien new world filled with statues and strange prayers.

My first days at school confirmed my worst fears and I found it to be a cold, unfriendly place filled with harsh, unsmiling strangers. Although the Head Master was actually a very kind man as I discovered later, unfortunately he had very little contact with the infant's classes. My first teacher was a very strict disciplinarian who made no allowance for the fact that my father had recently died. It was a completely unfriendly environment for a lively five year old and my natural exuberance was quickly suppressed. I didn't know how to behave or what was expected of me but I soon learned you were not allowed to talk and too many questions were frowned upon.

The classrooms were drab and very little natural light found its way in through the high, narrow windows. My impression of God as a harsh and forbidding bully who was not to be trusted was quickly reinforced by the teachers who constantly told us five year olds that God was always watching us and if we were naughty children and died we would go straight into the fires of hell! After the first week of being taken to school by my sister I had to walk home alone and I was extra careful as I crossed the roads in case I should be run over and go straight into those horrible fires which, the teacher assured us, never went out!

To look at, I was a plain little child, small and slight, with a freckly complexion and dead straight hair. I also had a tendency to say exactly what I thought, a trait which needless to say, didn't endear me to the teacher! It was my misfortune to sit in front of an angelic looking girl with long blonde ringlets. Unfortunately her character didn't match her appearance and she quickly cottoned on to an amusing little game at my expense. She poked me in the back and when I turned round she smiled angelically at the teacher who glared at me, shouting: "Turn round you! How many times do I have to tell you?" This was followed by a swift stinging slap and I soon learned it was pointless to argue and I often had to go and stand in the corner whilst my sweet faced tormenter sniggered behind her hand.

One incident stands out as an occasion of abject humiliation and shame. As usual I had been blamed for talking when 'angel face' poked me in the back and I was made to stand out in front of the class. The teacher slapped my legs so hard I cried and wet myself with fear. I can still remember the laughter of the other children as they watched the puddle spreading on the bare floorboards and the sneer of contempt on the teacher's face.

It is hard to believe that things have changed so drastically. I can only imagine the uproar if a teacher treated a five year old child in such a harsh manner these days; it would cause a public outcry but in the early fifties, it was accepted as normal discipline and my mother never made any complaints to the school. In fact when I told her, I didn't get much sympathy as she was of the opinion commonly held then that if you were disciplined in school you must have deserved it; in fact I don't remember her ever going near the school. I realised in later years that she had a fear of people in authority and hated confrontation of any kind. Unfortunately I had the same teacher for two years and this harsh treatment at such an early age only served to foster a rebellious streak in me and a resentment of authority figures. I was so miserable in my first couple of years at school that every day was a penance and once I learned to read, I began to use books as a means of escaping the misery and began to inhabit a world of make-believe and fantasy in order to cope with the emotional pain. The weekends were a welcome break from the harsh words and slaps of my teacher.

I had a couple of aunts who were very kind to me. One was my Dad's sister Aunty Teresa who shared his zany sense of humour. I would often call in to visit her on my way home from school and she would ply me with home made cakes and funny stories. One day I called there after school as usual but when I knocked on the door I was shocked to find it opened by a grim faced policeman.

"I'm sorry lass, you can't come in here. Go along home" he said. I knew instinctively that something terrible had happened and I couldn't understand why he refused to let me in or tell me where Aunty Teresa was. I ran home quickly to tell my mother what had happened but she brushed my questions aside and refused to talk about it. Later that night I was horrified to overhear that my Aunt had committed suicide by gassing herself. The thought of that kindly, jolly soul lying there on a cold kitchen floor with her head in the gas oven haunted me and for months my dreams were filled with terrifying images. I felt sick with fear; who would be next? I didn't have to wait very long to find out.

CHAPTER TWO

Pandora's Box

Is there no balm in Gilead?
Why then is there no healing
for the wounds of my people?
(Jeremiah 8: 22)

"Come along ladies. Try your luck. Win a doll for the little one!" The jolly man behind the hoopla stall called out, as we wandered around the fairground, mesmerised by all the wonderful sights and smells. We couldn't afford holidays, but once or twice a year Mum took me to Blackpool or Morecambe for a day trip. Aunty Bell, Mum's sister always came with us and we enjoyed strolling along the seafront eating candy floss or toffee apples before a visit to the funfair which was the highlight of the day. Then we'd make our way to our favourite cafe for tea before heading off to the station to catch the last train home. Aunty Bell was lots of fun and we were guaranteed a good laugh and a wonderful day out in her company. Tired but happy, we'd board the train laden with sticks of rock and fluffy toys we had won at the fairground if we'd had a lucky day.

Aunty Bell, who only had one son spoilt me and always made a great fuss of me and she and my mother were very close. Our regular day trips were something which I looked forward to eagerly and no sooner had we got back from one than I was pestering my mother: "When are we going again?" One morning I was woken by a persistent knocking on our door. I heard my mother cry out, "Oh No!" and I quickly ran downstairs, heart racing to find her in floods of tears. My Uncle Bill had just informed her that her dear sister Bell had suffered a massive brain haemorrhage and died during the night. My worst fears came to pass as yet another special person in my life died without warning and my fear of Mum dying intensified. I became even more insecure and my dreams were peopled with monsters. I was afraid to go to bed in case anybody else died whilst I was asleep.

Fear and insecurity tightened their grip around me. It was dangerous to love people because they could just die without warning. Deep roots of insecurity took hold and I withdrew further into a secret world inside my head where I was in control and nobody could hurt me. If there was an all powerful God, He was not to be trusted and as the years passed, I developed a hard outer shell to protect myself, hiding my real feelings behind a mask of insolence and indifference.

Although my mother never went to church, she was a

woman of prayer. But she had grown up believing that religion was 'private' and once when I found her kneeling by her bed in prayer she was most embarrassed. "I didn't know you prayed Mum" I said awkwardly. She mumbled something about Catholics not being the only ones who prayed and scrambled to her feet. She was a very honest person and she taught me that no matter how poor we were it was wrong to steal or cheat in any way. I know now that many of the things she said to me were direct quotations from the bible.

"You must be stupid!" my friends would mock if a shop-keeper gave me too much change and I took it back at once. They would justify dishonesty by saying: 'The shopkeeper's got more money than you.' But my mother's words: "Honesty is the best policy" rang in my ears and I felt compelled to return the extra money. The trouble was incidents like these only intensified my sense of being an oddball who was different from the other kids, a bit of a misfit. I was actually a bit of a loner with a vivid imagination and I could occupy myself quite happily for hours as long as I had a book to read and as soon as I was old enough I joined the local library. I used to spend hours in there and my love of books probably stems from the fact that we didn't own a television until I was in my teens when my brother gave us his old one. Anybody who read a lot was considered 'weird' and so I was careful not to let my friends know how much I loved reading.

I spent most of my life pretending to be somebody else; trying to fit in with what I thought other people wanted me to be. I was afraid that if people knew what I was really like they'd reject me and I became an abject people-pleaser. As well as reading, my other great pleasure was the cinema and my mother and I would go along two or three times a week to enjoy the latest offering from Hollywood or Elstree Studios. We particularly enjoyed thrillers and murder mysteries although westerns were good too with their rugged scenery and the only films my mother didn't like were musicals; she said the plots were totally implausible and the sight of somebody suddenly breaking into song in unbelievable situations was just silly, a view which I share to this day.

My interest in religion was another thing I was careful to hide from my friends. We were often taken to Mass during the week in the church which was right next door to our school. I sensed something special in there and the sanctuary light and lingering smell of incense and candles gave it an air of sanctity. Although I didn't understand sanctity, I just knew that this place was unlike anywhere else and often crept in unnoticed after school. I was fascinated by the enormous crucifix which hung over the altar and the numerous statues of various saints. As our parish was dedicated to the Sacred Heart, there was a large statue portraying Jesus with His heart exposed which I was particularly drawn to. I also liked the statue of the smiling man in a brown habit holding the little Jesus, who I learned was St. Anthony of Padua. As I gazed into the gentle face an inexplicable sadness swept over me and I wished that I could be held like the infant Jesus in somebody's strong arms.

I believe the Lord had his hand on my life even then

because I remember the first time I heard the account of the Passion of Christ. I must have been about eight years old and I listened with mounting horror to the account of Christ's suffering. When it came to the part where the crowd taunted him when he was on the cross, I was most indignant and could barely stop myself from springing up and shouting: "Get down and bash 'em Lord!" just like we would do at the cinema when Flash Gordon was faced by Ming the Merciless! Even at that age I believed that Jesus was the Son of God and that He was a very special and good person. Of course I didn't think He could possibly love me as I thought He only loved the good kids and I felt sad because I knew I was definitely not one of them! It seemed that no matter how hard I tried, I always seemed to end up doing something wrong and getting into trouble.

There was a side of my nature that I was careful to hide from others; for instance in our spare bedroom I made a little altar on an old washstand, carefully placing a jam jar containing wild flowers before a picture of Jesus. I would have died from embarrassment if any of my friends had seen it. In front of them I was most irreverent at times, and took delight in amusing them whilst we were in Mass, although deep down I felt ashamed and uncomfortable with myself. Only in later years did I learn the truth of the words: "To thine own self be true." But this was all part of the people pleasing, the desperation to be accepted by others and not to be considered different in any way. The trouble was, I was not really happy behaving in this way and I began to despise myself more and more.

"Deep and wide, deep and wide, there's a fountain flowing

deep and wide......" The prim little organist struggled to keep up with the enthusiastic Sunday school teacher Mr. Dodds.

"Come on boys and girls, let's show everyone how big God's love is!" he said, as he flung his arms to the sky. He was a dear sweet man with lots of patience and I believe his greatest desire was to instill in us a love for the bible. "Remember boys and girls" he said, "this book is the Holy Word of God and it will never let you down." He was so earnest but for the most part, we were largely oblivious to the Holy Word of God and just wanted to have a couple of hours of fun on wet Sunday afternoons. I was with my friends in the little Gospel Hall at the end of our street, and to be honest we were not much interested in the height or depth of God's love! Our sole reason for being there was to collect enough 'points' to qualify for the Sunday school picnic. I had sneaked in along with my Protestant friends and was anxious in case Mr. Dodds discovered I was a Catholic and threw me out! "Do you think he'll know?" I asked my friend anxiously. She looked me up and down thoughtfully before declaring confidently: "Nah, you don't look like one! I was relieved to hear this and didn't stop to wonder what she thought Catholics looked like! I was also terrified that somebody would spot me going in to the Gospel Hall and tell the parish priest.

In those days we didn't go into non-Catholic churches and we were taught that only those of the 'one, true faith' would get to Heaven. I never did believe that and as I didn't hold out much hope of getting to Heaven anyway, I wasn't too worried about associating with these good hearted folk.

What did frighten me was the thought that the Parish Priest, the Canon, would get to hear of it and then I would be in big trouble. I was certainly more afraid of him than I was of God. Ecumenism didn't feature on the agenda in those days, and certainly not on the Canon's! We used to go to confession on Saturday mornings and there would be a long queue outside the door where the kindly young assistant priest heard confessions. Outside the door where the dreaded Canon sat glowering, the pews were empty. After some time, the Canon would fling open the door of the confessional, point menacingly at us and thunder, "You, you and you! Get over here this very minute!" The unfortunate ones who had caught his eye went with fear and trembling to kneel in the pew until it was their turn to face the inquisition! It was a most unfortunate experience to have to go to the Canon for confession and certainly did nothing to convince us of God's love. In fact, if God was anything like Canon we would rather not go to Heaven, especially if it meant meeting up with him again! Whatever the alternative to Heaven was, it surely couldn't be much worse than being grilled by the Canon? He certainly succeeded in instilling the fear of God into us!

Once a year the Sunday school classes piled into a ramshackle old coach which took us to a small town about thirty miles away, although we might have been on a trip to the moon judging by the level of excitement generated. Once we arrived at the field where we were to spend the day, we poured out of the coach to the horror of Miss Galbraith, the timid little organist. It was a very brave service she performed for God, second only no doubt to a stint in the mission field!

"Children, please calm down. Remember you are God's children, not a herd of buffalo." This generated even more hysteria as we whooped and hollered all over the field by the river where we were to have our 'feast'.

Each child received a brown paper bag containing a couple of curled-up cheese sandwiches, a fairy cake and a small bottle of fizzy lemonade to wash it down, but to us it was a banquet. Because none of our families had cars, it was a rare treat to go on such an outing and we looked forward to it for months. As soon as it was over, of course, spiritual pursuits lost their appeal until next year! Although I actually enjoyed the weekly slide shows with their stirring tales of Moses, Jonah, Joshua and Daniel, I would never have dared attend Sunday school alone for fear of being called a 'Holy Joe' and so when my friends stopped going, so did I.

When I was seven, I made my First Holy Communion, a big event in the life of any little Catholic child. Of course I couldn't understand the significance of it, but I knew it was something very special. It was also something else to be feared too because we were told that it was a sin to chew the host and we must let it dissolve on our tongue. But horror of horrors, what if, God forbid, it stuck to the roof of your mouth? We were on no account to touch it with our sinful little fingers and I lived in terror of committing a 'mortal sin' by accidentally getting it stuck in my teeth! A mortal sin meant I would be immediately cast into Hell should I die before I made it to confession.

Little wonder with such teaching that I thought of God as a

terrifying bully who ruled the whole world with a rod of iron whose main desire was to cast as many people into Hell as possible. Apparently he even had legions of angels spying on us and reporting back to Him so that you could never do anything without God knowing about it. What a travesty, and a far cry from the truth, but for a seven year old child brought up in the fifties, it was a pretty commonly held belief. Sadly, it is a belief which is still held by people of a certain age. No wonder so many people turned their back on religion with such distorted ideas of God.

When the special day dawned in June when I was to make my First Holy Communion, I put on my borrowed white dress, fastened my little white sandals and set off down the road to church all alone. My mother would not come with me as I think she was afraid she might be embarrassed, unaccustomed as she was to Catholic masses. And no other member of my family came to see me on my great day. Although I put on a brave face, I felt sad and embarrassed that I was the only child there who had no family members milling around, taking photos and making a fuss of them. I sat there squirming in my seat at the special breakfast laid on for us and made my escape as soon as possible.

As the years passed, the dreaded 11-plus exam drew near. This exam was held to decide which children should attend the local grammar school, whilst the rest were sent to the secondary modern school as they were called then. Although I loved reading, writing essays and most other subjects, I absolutely hated maths. This was really my weakest subject and had it not been for the kindly attentions of my headmaster, Mr. Leonard, I would not have had a chance of passing the exam. But Mr. Leonard, or Barney, as he was affectionately known, spotted my weakness and spent hours coaching me separately in maths. God has put some special people in my life, and Barney Leonard was one of them. A gentle, unassuming man, he was known to be both fair but strict. If you were on the level, you had no problems with Mr. Leonard but heaven help you if you lied to him or tried to pull the wool over his eyes. For some reason he seemed to like me and often told me that if I behaved myself, I could go far in life. I suspect he had recognised my rebellious streak and was trying to warn me that my behaviour might one day get me into serious trouble. Unfortunately, I failed to heed him and I was to take many wrong turnings and hit many dead ends before I got back on track.

During the month of May the results of the '11 plus' exam arrived and I was actually dismayed to learn that I had passed, which meant I could attend the convent school. At the time I didn't appreciate the opportunity which was being offered to me and I just wanted to go to the local secondary modern school, along with most of my class-mates.

"Margaret, you are a bright girl." Mr. Leonard told me. "But you have a tendency to gravitate towards the wrong sort of people and if you're not careful you will get into trouble. Please take up the place at the convent; I promise you, you will not regret it." And so after much persuasion from Barney Leonard, I decided to give the convent school a try. "Do your best Margaret and behave yourself!" My mother's words rang in my ears as I walked nervously up the long tree lined drive of the convent school, feeling very self conscious in my new gabardine coat and beret with its fancy metal badge. The convent school had originally been for fee paying pupils but now served as a Catholic grammar school for girls. Because my mother was a widow, she was given a grant towards the cost of the school uniform and so it had to last me for as long as possible even if it meant that my gabardine coat was not far from my ankles. Because I tried to make it look shorter by bunching it up around the middle with the belt, I looked more like a sack of potatoes than an smart convent schoolgirl and was embarrassed as I pedalled out of the street on my shiny new bike trying desperately to keep my coat from getting caught up in the chain. I know that my mother made many sacrifices in order to buy me extras such as a hockey stick and tennis racquet and a special box of paints which were not covered by the grant and I am grateful to her now although I didn't appreciate it at the time.

The atmosphere at the convent school was completely different from primary school: it was far less boring and restrictive and I soon settled in. The teachers did their best to instill good manners and ladylike behaviour into us - with varying degrees of success. In addition we were taught to 'speak correctly' which didn't go down too well with me. I had a chip on my shoulder about 'posh' people, it was bad enough having to run the gauntlet each day through our local council estate wearing my ill-fitting school uniform amid taunts of: "You think you're posh now don't you!" I didn't want to be accused of 'talking posh' as well! When we had elocution lessons I steadfastly and stubbornly refused to amend my diction and in fact deliberately spoke with a broad Lancashire accent! This was typical of me, refusing to conform and rebelling against those in authority. My years at the primary school had embittered me and I had become a very angry person ready to lash out at the slightest provocation.

My first few years at the convent school were happy and productive and I managed to stay in the top five as far as exam results were concerned, with the exception of maths which I hated. Maths lessons became unbearable when a supply teacher was appointed who made fun of my feeble performance, humiliating me before the whole class and in sheer desperation I began to play truant. Each morning I left for school at the usual time then went straight to my oldest sister's house. The first time I turned up on her doorstep in tears, Betty took pity on me and let me stay, with the warning that it mustn't happen again. But when I turned up every morning she couldn't find it in her heart to turn me away, so I spent the days at her house arriving home at around the time I was due in from school.

This went on for about six weeks until finally the dreaded 'school board man' caught up with me. It was his job to chase up truants such as me and my heart sank as my mother invited him in. "I think you must be mistaken," she said. "Margaret has never missed a day at school." Soon the whole sorry tale came tumbling out. The officer was sympathetic when I explained the problem with the supply teacher, saying that I should have told somebody about this from the start. I went back to school the next day and poured out my heart to the headmistress who was very understanding. Whatever she said to that teacher did the trick and from that day on she left me alone. One thing I learnt from this was that you can't teach a person anything by humiliating them.

In complete contrast to the Maths teacher, my English teacher was an absolute treasure and as it was my favourite subject, we had an immediate rapport. She arranged for our class to see 'A Midsummer Night's Dream' at a theatre in Blackpool and although I dearly wanted to go I didn't put my name forward. Miss Horton rightly guessed the reason was because my mother couldn't afford the cost of a ticket, plus the coach fare. Taking me aside and telling me not to say a word to anyone, she paid for the trip out of her own pocket. I have never forgotten that kindness. She was another special teacher that God put in my life and I was sad when she eventually moved on.

By now I was in my early teens and the so-called 'Swinging Sixties' were in full swing. Along with all the hormonal changes, a strange restlessness set in when I was about fourteen and whereas I had previously been quite happy to stay at home in the evenings listening to the radio and doing my homework, I now wanted to go out at nights with some of my secondary school friends. One weekend I met a new crowd of girls through a mutual friend and I was invited to join them at a dance in a local church hall. It seemed harmless enough so I went along and for the first couple of Saturdays just enjoyed the music and watching the others dance - I was much too shy to dance myself. One Saturday night I heard loud laughter coming from the ladies toilets. Curiosity got the better of me and I went to see what all the noise was about; somebody was certainly enjoying themselves. I was intrigued when three girls staggered out clutching a bottle of wine.

"Want a swig?" one of them giggled. When I hesitated she said: "Why don't you just stay home with your Mam if you're frightened to have a bit of fun!" Stung by her taunts I snatched the bottle and promptly drank the contents in one go. The girls were speechless and not too happy that I had finished off their booze. "That'll teach them!" I thought. Before long the drink took effect and the sensation was enjoyable. I felt on top of the world as I swaggered back into the dance hall with a new found confidence. I had taken the first step on what was to become for me a slippery slope, and my life took an immediate downward turn. Little did I know it then, but I had just opened up Pandora's Box.

From then on I began to live a double life; during the week I was a good little convent schoolgirl and at the weekend I became a different person, drinking and going around with a wild bunch. I had a part-time job by now to finance the drinking and smoking and somehow my mother never realised what was going on, although she quizzed me closely on Saturday nights when I got home. Fortunately for me she had a very poor sense of smell and I was a good actress so I managed to fool her.

At school it seemed as though I was living in a parallel universe, the nuns were so out of touch with what was happening in a rapidly changing society and still ran the school pretty much as they did in the Thirties. One morning at assembly our head, Sr. Ursula, a particularly ladylike nun stood with her lips pursed and her head bowed and we knew she must have something serious on her mind.

"My dear girls" she said solemnly: "It has come to my notice that some of you have been behaving in a disgraceful manner in public places." She paused for effect and my heart sank: "Oh no!" I thought. "Somebody has seen me drunk in town and reported me." She continued: "Yes, I have heard that some of you have been walking up Dalton Road eating ice creams whilst still wearing your school uniforms!" She was horrified and it was all I could do not to laugh out loud, it seemed so ridiculous. Thank goodness she didn't see what really went on in Dalton Road on a Saturday night with some of her pupils; then she would have had something to be shocked about!

Inevitably as the drinking progressed, my school work began to suffer and as the G.C.E.s loomed nearer I became increasingly reckless. Unfortunately the results of my 'mock' 'O' Levels were excellent, which made me cocky and gave me a false sense of security.

"You'll do well Margaret, you're a bright girl." My Head Teacher was convinced I was headed for university and encouraged me to revise for the exams. I found the old test papers we used fairly easy so I thought I'd breeze through the exams. Unlike my classmates who were working hard revising for the exams, I was out having fun and I paid the price. Instead of studying I spent my free time going to the dance hall or hanging around coffee bars. Not that I had any interest in going to university. Nobody in my family had ever been and so it didn't really cross my mind that I could go, I thought it was for 'posh' people. All I wanted to do was get out of school as fast as possible and earn some money to provide the means to keep up the wild lifestyle I'd adopted.

I was alone in the house the day the exam results arrived and I nonchalantly opened the envelope. My heart sank when I saw that out of the six exams I'd taken I had passed only two and I dreaded telling my mother. I felt ashamed when I thought of the sacrifices she'd made in order to send me to the Convent School. I had thrown away a wonderful opportunity because I was too busy having what I thought was a good time and was too short sighted to see what lay ahead for somebody with no qualifications. I seemed to bounce from one crisis to another and I soon found out the hard way that leaving school was not such a good idea after all.

Although the Headmistress tried to persuade me to re-sit my exams, I was too stubborn and proud, insisting that it was time I left school and started to earn some money. I was keen to get out into the real world but little did I know I was jumping from the frying pan straight into the fire!

CHAPTER THREE

Looking for Love

You will forget the shame
of your youth ...
(Isaiah 54: 4)

I wasted no time in leaving school and finding a job. My intention was to take anything that was going to earn some money. I had vague notions of journalism although I hadn't got a clue what qualifications were required and wouldn't have known where to start. I was incredibly naive, thinking that if you were reasonably intelligent you were bound to get a good job. It was just a matter of time and finding the niche which suited you. How pathetically unrealistic I was and I soon discovered that the number of jobs I was actually qualified for was very limited. I didn't even have shorthand and typing skills, so factory and shop jobs were all that were offered me and reality soon set in.

The thought of spending my life in a dead end job was soul

destroying but I was too proud to listen to take the advice I was offered at the job centre – go back to school and re-sit my exams. Not me, oh no, I wanted to have a good time so I took a job in a shop with little thought for the future. Saturday night and the next drunken session at the dance hall were my number one priority; that and finding a boyfriend. Up until that point I hadn't gone out with any-body except for the odd night at the pictures as my mother wasn't happy about me 'taking up with boys' as she put it. I was ripe for a fall and easy pickings for the first person who said 'I love you.'

The shop was a family owned hardware store and I was sent to work in the fancy goods department. I enjoyed the work and discovered a talent for selling. Before long the boss offered me a pay rise of ten shillings (about fifty pence) which brought my total pay to three pounds and fifty pence a week.

I worked with a lady called Doreen who was very amusing with a lively fund of stories and jokes which carried us over the quiet times. I noticed she seemed to grow more jovial as the day wore on. When I got back after my lunch break Doreen seemed to be full of high spirits but what I didn't realise was that the spirits came out of a bottle! She was in the habit of sending me across to the off license to buy her a miniature bottle of whiskey saying it was good for her circulation. With hindsight, I realise poor Doreen was an alcoholic. I heard some years later she had met a rather horrible end, having fallen into an open fire whilst drunk. She was always very kind to me and I was sorry to hear she had died so tragically.

Saturday night was dance night, the night to go looking for booze and men in that order. By this time I was drinking heavily and if my mother had seen my behaviour around the dance halls she would have been appalled. One favourite haunt had a reputation for being rough and the local toughs used to hang out there. Every week there were fights and the police were often called in to restore order. When fights broke out I would join in, throwing chairs into the melee and wading into the thick of it. Despite being less than five feet tall and slightly built, I became very aggressive when drunk, taking on all comers.

One night I came close to spending the night in the cells. One of the local toughs was suddenly grabbed by a burly police sergeant just as we were leaving the dance hall. For once this guy had not been involved in any trouble and as I've always hated injustice of any kind, I gave the sergeant a sharp clout with my umbrella! He wheeled around and grabbed me. "If you don't want to join him lassie" he said, referring to my friend who had by now been thrown into the back of the police van, "you'd better get home right now, or your mother will be getting a visit from us." The mention of my mother had the effect of sobering me up pretty quickly. I remembered how upset she had been when the school board man had called at the house because of my truancy. To be told that I'd been arrested would have broken her heart.

On another occasion when a local thug attacked a man in a pub, I was outraged and proceeded to hit the attacker over the head with a bottle! Fortunately it didn't do him much harm and had the effect of stopping the attack. However, he threatened to 'get' me when he had the chance and in fact he chased me one night up the street brandishing a knife. I sought refuge in a pub or perhaps I might not be here to tell the tale as he was definitely psychotic. I was totally reckless and careless of my own safety and drink got me into some pretty nasty situations. Once when I was in Brighton I waded in to defend an old tramp who was being assaulted by a gang of youths. Fortunately somebody came to our rescue and sent the thugs packing but I could have been badly hurt. Looking back now I believe that God was watching over me!

My mother was very strict and wouldn't allow me to bring boys home which I'm sure was her way of protecting me. Instead of protecting me however, it had the effect of driving me into some dangerous situations. Very few people had cars in those days and it was quite a novelty to get a lift home from the dance and one guy who had his own car often took me home and sometimes we would go for a ride in the country at weekends. However this all had to be done in secret and we would meet up at a pre-arranged place so my mother didn't see him. His name was Terry and he was five or six years older than me. I'm sure if my mother had allowed me to bring him home she would have liked him and things might have been very different.

I had also been secretly dating my boss's son. It all started at a staff night out when I had a bit too much to drink and he gave me a lift home. He was unlike anyone I had ever been out with. To me he seemed sophisticated and charming, he was quite a bit older than me and I was flattered by his attentions. I am mortified now at the thought of how naive I was and how I let him use me.

One weekend he took me to his parent's house when they were away. It was a lovely big house close to the beach and I was very impressed. I knew in my heart that this was all wrong, after all why was he sneaking around behind his parents' back? Also he insisted that no-one must know about us but I was so bowled over by his attentions I readily agreed. That weekend, he plied me with drink and I ended up sleeping with him. I had never done anything like that before and I felt miserable and deeply ashamed of myself when I sobered up. I could hardly face my mother when I got home. I know now that I had very low self-esteem and was so desperate for affection that I allowed myself to be used by the first man who told me he loved me.

Just before Christmas he ditched me. I was totally humiliated and spent a miserable Christmas as I faced the fact that I had been nothing more than a brief fling, something to amuse him while the weather was too bad for rock climbing! This only served to increase my feelings of self-loathing. It was very difficult to carry on working at the shop as though nothing had happened but I didn't want to lose my job and was terrified the truth would come out. I tried to put him out of my mind but I had been badly hurt and began to drink even more in an attempt to escape the sense of shame and humiliation.

It was Valentine's Day 1964, and I went to a dance in the local Territorial Army hall. Somebody had gone to a lot of trouble to transform the drab old building, decorating it with paper hearts and flowers and there was a 'buzz' in the air. A local group belted out all the latest hits and what with the heat and the drink, I was soon feeling the worse for wear.

"I've missed you" said my old friend Terry. I hadn't seen him for ages and was glad of his easy company. He was very undemanding and didn't ask too many questions. We danced together most of the evening and the strains of the last dance lingered in the air as we walked out into the cold February night. Buying fish and chips on the way home we turned our collars up against the relentless drizzle. "Too bad the old car broke down", laughed Terry. "Never mind, the fresh air will sober us up!"

When we got near my home we took a short cut through the grounds of a local school. Because my mother wouldn't allow me to bring boyfriends home, Terry and I took refuge in the school porch to say goodnight. As it was so cold and wet we were glad of the shelter offered by the deep porch, besides it was a good place to eat our fish and chips. Up until that time, Terry had always been a perfect gentleman and I suppose it must have been a combination of alcohol and opportunity that made him lose his inhibitions. I was still hurt by my recent rejection and once again, full of booze and desperate to be loved, I allowed myself to be used. I woke up the next morning with a sick feeling in the pit of my stomach and tried to remember what had happened the night before. Whatever it was, once more I felt dirty and ashamed of myself.

In spite of my behaviour I continued to go to Mass each Sunday, usually in the evening as I was too hung-over in the mornings. I never doubted the existence of God, but I was sure He wouldn't have much time for the likes of me. I couldn't seem to keep the rules, and was sure He only loved nice girls.

As the weeks went by I began to feel unwell, especially in the mornings when I felt nauseous. When I mentioned it to Doreen during one of our tea breaks, she quizzed me closely and in a doom laden voice announced: "Sounds to me like you're pregnant." I was utterly aghast, and for once in my life I was speechless. What could I say? I felt like running outside and throwing myself under a bus. The rest of that day was spent in a haze of misery and fear. What could I do? Who could I turn to? I was shattered. Why did this have to happen to me when many of the girls I knew had been very promiscuous but they weren't pregnant? Trust me! It seemed to be the story of my life; any wrong I did I always had to pay for. A 'one-night' stand had had devastating consequences for me. One of my mother's favourite sayings sprang to mind; "Beware your sins will find you out." Well, they certainly had no trouble locating me!

The thought of having a baby was still something vague and far away, my immediate worry was what would my mother say? I couldn't tell her, it would kill her. She was not in very good health and had suffered enough problems in her life. I bitterly regretted the hurt this would cause her; she didn't deserve any more heartache. She'd done her best to keep me on the right track but somehow there was something deeply wrong with me, a great void inside me. I never felt loved and I suppose I went looking for 'love' in all the wrong places.

Looking back, I am amazed that I managed to carry on as I did; after all, I was a rather immature seventeen-year-old, less than a year out of school and bearing this awful secret alone. In the early stages I never gave much thought to the baby, it still seemed unreal, like a bad dream. But this was definitely one thing that would not go away by ignoring it!

As the weeks went by my one aim was to conceal my expanding waistline. Fortunately the overall supplied for work was very loose fitting and hid it well. At the time baggy sweaters were fashionable and these allowed me to carry on for nearly six months without anyone guessing my secret. The pressure on me was enormous and some days I thought my head would burst with the effort of pretending things were normal. I hadn't seen much of Terry since the night of the dance, but I knew I would have to tell him about the baby as soon as possible. He hadn't been around the usual haunts so I decided to go to his house and confront him with the news. At first when I told him, he was shocked but made no effort to deny it. However, the next time I went to his house, his mother opened the door and made it quite plain that as far as she was concerned, it was nothing to do with her son and I was not welcome at their house again. She closed the door firmly in my face. As I walked away from her door I was in a terrible state of confusion. What did she mean 'it was nothing to do with her son?' I knew only too well that it was but I was too young and immature to argue so I walked miserably home.

My mind was in a turmoil and I just wished that I could die, that seemed to be the only way out. I wondered how many tablets it would take to kill myself and whether aspirins would work.

The next time I saw Terry he looked decidedly uncomfortable when I mentioned the baby. He shrugged and made it quite clear I was on my own; he just didn't want to know. I felt utterly humiliated. I don't know what I had expected from him but it certainly had never crossed my mind he would react like this. I felt so alone and wretched that if there had been a bridge nearby I would have jumped off it.

Things finally came to a head towards the end of August when I felt so miserable and lonely I couldn't keep this secret any longer. By now I was six months pregnant and I had to tell somebody in my family so I decided to confide in my oldest sister, Betty. She insisted that we go and tell my mother right away and as we walked through the hot dusty streets I felt more and more miserable. How could I do this to my mother after all she'd done for me?

Betty walked in first and I stumbled in after her. "What on earth's the matter?" I let Betty tell Mum, I just couldn't find the words. Mum broke down and wept. I thought she would never stop crying but after she managed to compose herself her reaction surprised me. She was very understanding and only became angry when I told her about Terry's attitude.

"That's typical Margaret" she said. "It's easy for the man to walk away, leaving the girl holding the baby. It's the old story. Once they've had their fun they leave you to face the music. Yes you were stupid and that's what you get for being drunk, but you're paying dearly for your mistake. And you'll keep on paying for the rest of your life."

When Betty left, my mother and I talked long into the night, probably more frankly than we had ever done before. With the selfishness of youth I had never realised what a difficult life my mother had had and from then on our relationship improved. I went to bed that night feeling a little happier I began to think seriously for the first time about the baby. Now that the worst was over – or so I thought – I imagined myself with a little baby in my arms or pushing a pram in the same park where I had spent so many happy hours with my dad. "I'll take him or her on the boating lake and we'll fish for minnows, just like I did with Dad." I told myself. I would be fine, after all I'd had plenty of experience baby-sitting my nephews and nieces. Would it be a boy or a girl, I wondered? I didn't mind just so long as it was healthy. I breathed a sigh of relief.

At last the truth was out and it hadn't been as bad as I'd feared. My mother had been very understanding and I was sure that with her help I would be able to look after my baby. Although I can't deny I was afraid of what lay ahead, I began to get used to the idea of having a baby and for the first time in months I slept well. My happiness however was short-lived and next morning as I was eating breakfast my mother dropped the bombshell.

CHAPTER FOUR

I Will Never Forget You

Can a mother forget her baby?
(Isaiah 49: 15)

"Of course you can't keep the baby. You'll have to have it adopted," my mother said as she poured my tea. "What do you mean?" I felt the first stirrings of alarm. "Well I can't bring up a baby at my age. You know I'm in poor health. How could I cope with that? And what would you live on? You'll have to go back to work; we can't live on fresh air." The cold blast of reality hit me like a ton of bricks.

"I'll look after the baby myself' I said. "How could you – you need money to live on Margaret" she said. "You've got to face facts." She was right of course. Without a job I would be penniless. In those days there was no government help for anybody in my position. The attitude was "You got yourself into this mess. Now get yourself out of it". As for being given a flat to live in and financial assistance, such an idea was laughable back then. As far as society was concerned the attitude was: "You clean up your own mess. You can't expect society to pay for your mistakes!" If your family couldn't help you then that was just too bad! Why should you expect the government to help you?

The term 'single parent' had not yet been coined and there was very little sympathy for unmarried mothers and certainly no financial assistance as there is today. There was still a stigma attached to illegitimacy and to become pregnant outside of marriage was shameful. You were a social outcast and the term 'bastard' was freely applied to babies born out of wedlock. It was very hypocritical actually; on the one hand it was the so-called "Swinging Sixties", with a more liberated attitude to sex: it was okay to sleep around as long as you took the pill but if you got pregnant, you ought to be ashamed of yourself. In other words, do what you like as long as you don't get caught. As for me, I would pay a very heavy price for my one-off drunken lapse. I felt deeply ashamed of myself and the perceived gap between me and God grew even greater.

The official title of the social worker assigned to me was the 'Moral Welfare Officer', implying that her job was looking after immoral people like me! Her office was on the top floor of a decrepit old building and I was apprehensive as I climbed the winding staircase. "It will probably be some old dragon who will give me a lecture," I thought as I reached the top of the stairs. I was out of breath and desperate to sit down and have a rest. Some rickety chairs arranged outside a glass paneled door, were already occupied by a number of scruffy looking people who looked as miserable as I felt. A smell of stale cabbage hung in the air and a pall of cigarette smoke added to the general gloom. I leaned wearily against the wall. Sunk as they were in their own gloom, nobody offered me a seat.

After a wretched hour spent leafing nervously through some tatty old magazines, I was ushered into a rather untidy room filled with well worn furniture and piles of dusty files. Mrs. Harcourt, the social worker smiled wearily and indicating a shabby armchair, told me to sit down. She was actually a kind, gentle person but I soon realised that beneath the angora and pearls was a very tough lady who was nobody's fool. She quickly gained my respect.

"Margaret, I know this is not easy for you but I am here to help you. There's a nice little mother and baby home just outside Kendal where you'll be taken good care of for six weeks until your baby's born. Then afterwards, you'll stay for another six weeks until it's time for the adoption. You do realise my dear what you are doing don't you?" she said. I broke down and wept. "I don't want to give my baby away."

She continued, "I'm sure you don't dear, but you know it will be for the best. What could you offer a child in your position? I know your mother is very upset about this too but she's just not able to take on such a big responsibility at her age. She has poor health Margaret and she couldn't possibly take care of a baby while you went out to work. She's raised seven children of her own and it would be unfair to put another burden on her. Besides, without a job, how could you possibly afford to take care of a child?

Please try to be brave and think of what's best for the baby."

She made some phone calls whilst I sat there in abject
misery. I didn't want to be brave. I just wanted to keep my
baby. Surely nobody would force me to give it up? "Once
they see it," I thought, "they're bound to let me keep it." The
thought of handing my baby over to strangers was
unbearable. "Please don't make me do this," I begged.

"I'm sorry dear, there really is no alternative. I've spoken to
Sister Marie and she will be expecting us on the 4th of
September." I was horrified; in less than a month I was
being shunted off to some place I didn't want to go to, to do
something I didn't want to do and I was utterly powerless.
I couldn't have felt worse if I'd been told I was going to be
executed.

The next few weeks flew past in a blur. My mother had of
course explained to my employers what had happened and
I know they were very sorry to lose me. Poor Doreen in the
meantime had been dismissed; she had apparently taken
one bottle of 'medicine' too many during working hours
and after being helped to the station, was poured onto the
train.

The day finally dawned when I was to be collected by Mrs.
Harcourt and taken to Brettargh Holt, the mother and baby
home. As I waited for the Social Worker to collect me I was
desperately hoping my mother would change her mind. I
know she was heartbroken as she said goodbye, she could
hardly look at me but she insisted I had to go. She told me
later how hard it had been for her to send me away but she
could see no alternative.

Throughout the journey Mrs. Harcourt did her utmost to put me at ease, chatting brightly about the lovely country-side and the fact that autumn would soon be upon us, even pointing out a roe deer bounding over a fence into the woods. For once I was indifferent to the beauty of the Lake District and the magnificent colours of autumn meant nothing to me. I sat there in a haze of misery and withdrew further and further into myself, hardly saying a word in response to Mrs. Harcourt's breezy chatter.

"You won't regret it, dear. I know it's not going to be easy for you but it's for the best, you'll see. Besides, you really have no alternative." That was the most sickening part, the fact that I had no say in something that would change my life forever. I might as well have been invisible for all that anybody listened to me. Important decisions had been made for me and as far as everybody was concerned, that was the end of the matter.

At last the car swung off the main road and entered a long sweeping drive lined with ancient oaks and beech trees. It was an imposing drive and as we swept around the bend I caught my first sight of Brettargh Holt which was to be my home for the next three months. The house was very old and quite beautiful and in different circumstances I would have been excited at the prospect of living in such gracious surroundings. As we climbed the steps leading to a huge oak door I felt sick and my heart was thumping wildly; I was tempted to run away, but where could I go with this tiny life growing daily within me. What did the future hold for either of us?

The tiny nun who opened the door was almost completely hidden by the old fashioned habit worn in those days. She spoke briefly with Mrs. Harcourt, who shook my hand, wished me well and quickly left. I stood there in the large hall with only the sombre ticking of an old clock breaking the silence. Sister Marie ushered me into a rather austere room which she referred to as the 'Green Room.' "Sit down, child" she said briskly. "Sister Felicity will be with you soon". The door opened once more and a much taller nun came in. "Come along, dear" she said, taking hold of both of my hands. She smiled at me and I promptly burst into tears. She didn't say a word, but somehow I knew she understood how I felt. There was no condemnation, only compassion in her eyes. Picking up my battered little suitcase, the kindly nun led me up the imposing staircase and showed me to my room. "You'll be sharing a room with Monica. I'm sure you'll get on just fine."

Sister Felicity explained that in this home, in order to preserve our anonymity, each girl was given a 'new name.' Many of the girls were Irish and had come to England to do their nursing training. They were deeply ashamed of their situation and went to great lengths to ensure their families wouldn't discover the truth and they jealously guarded their identity. The name I was given was 'Shirley' and for the next three months I would have to learn to answer to a strange name. This shows how shameful illegitimacy was. Things have certainly changed since those days when 'unmarried mothers' were shunted off to institutions and given fictitious names! But even worse things had taken place in earlier times, when some unfortunate souls who found themselves pregnant were incarcerated in mental hospitals, sometimes for the rest of their lives!

At Brettargh Holt we were all allocated particular daily duties; this was your 'job' and you took it very seriously, or at least were supposed to. I certainly did because I was assigned to the milk kitchen where all the babies' bottles were made up and it was vital that everything was kept scrupulously clean. Actually I soon realised I was quite privileged to work there as there were many less pleasant jobs such as scrubbing out the toilets or working in the laundry. Only mothers-to-be were allowed to work in the milk kitchen or nursery. Once we'd had our babies, we were discouraged from spending too much time in the nursery area, knowing that soon we would have to give our babies away to strangers, never to see them again.

Sister Marie Jude was my 'boss' and I soon grew very close to her. She had the most remarkable grey eyes I have ever seen, full of compassion. Although I never heard her utter a harsh word, anybody who tried to pull the wool over her eyes soon discovered she was nobody's fool and a frown was enough to discourage any bad behaviour. She was a trained midwife and it was my hope she would be on duty when it came time to deliver my baby. The other nun who delivered the babies was Sister Marie who was a doctor. Although she was less than five feet tall, most people felt intimidated by her but once you got to know her it was soon apparent she was really very kind beneath the rather stern exterior. Perhaps she cultivated that persona to compensate for her lack of height. To be fair to the sisters, I never experienced the cruelty and unkindness reportedly experienced by others in similar institutions.

Monica who I shared a room with was considerably older than me. She was very well spoken, and I discovered she taught at a finishing school in Switzerland. In fact she was a delight to share a room with and was very kind to me. I think she realised just how nervous I was. I loved to listen to her tales of how the poor little rich girls behaved and gained some insight into how the 'other half' lived. It seemed that sex and drink featured largely on the curriculum - unofficially of course - which surprised me as I had imagined such 'posh' schools to be dull places full of prim and proper goody-goodies. As I said, I was very naive.

The girls in the home were a mixed bunch; some were obviously from well-to-do families whilst others were from very poor homes. Most of us were young, although there were a couple of older married women who perhaps had had an extra-marital fling. These women tended to keep to themselves whilst we younger ones spent most of our free time together. The fact that we were all pregnant in difficult circumstances was a great leveller and on the whole people did their best to get on with each other. We didn't have much choice really, we just had to make the best of a bad situation and as well as the tears, there was lots of laughter as well.

"What's the matter? This place is like a morgue!" I hadn't been there very long and the moment I went down to breakfast one morning, I sensed an air of sadness in the dining room. Monica put a finger to her lips. "Sh!" she said; "Bridie's baby is leaving today. They're coming to pick him up at ten o'clock and Bridie's been crying all night."

This was my first experience of what it was like when one of the babies was taken away by the adoptive parents. A pall of gloom hung over the whole house and during my time in Brettargh Holt there was great sadness each time one of the girls had to hand over her baby, I guess because we all knew that one day it would be our turn. Nowadays we know about the importance of a mother and child bonding in the first days and weeks of a baby's life, but back in the Sixties nobody seemed to realise the terrible impact that parting with a child you had carried in your womb for nine months then nurtured and loved for six weeks might have on both mother and baby.

However, apart from these sad times when one of the babies left, we had plenty of laughs and there was lots of good natured banter. I suppose it was a bit like being in prison, you could either spend the whole time being miserable or make an effort to adapt and try to see the funny side of things.

Our days were quite regimented and after early morning mass we filed into the dining room for breakfast. This was the place where mail was distributed and we looked forward eagerly to getting mail from home. The nuns scored out our real names on the envelopes and hastily wrote in our pseudonyms. After breakfast we went off to our various tasks before meeting up again at eleven for tea, biscuits and the all important chat. Time passed surprisingly quickly and with so many feeds to prepare each day I was kept busy in the milk kitchen.

Weekends were free and occasionally a group of us

would take a bus into the nearby town of Kendal, where we wandered around the shops looking at the baby wear and knowing that soon somebody else would be choosing clothes for our babies. I bought a cheap imitation wedding ring in Woolworth's which I wore to cover my shame and embarrassment, although it must have been obvious to all when confronted by six or seven young girls who were heavily pregnant that we were from 'the unmarried Mothers home' down the road. At times we became aware of people staring at us and occasionally heard their unkind taunts. It was a humiliating experience and cast a shadow over our little trips. I was usually glad to get back to the safety of Brettargh Holt. At least there we were all in the same boat.

My baby was due on the twenty-first of November and on the night of Friday the nineteenth I went to bed feeling decidedly odd. It was strange that we were not given much information about childbirth; after all it was a little late to start being coy about such things. I was incredibly ignorant and there was no such thing as ante-natal classes. We had to work right up until the birth and many of us didn't know what to expect. When I had asked Sister Marie Jude "How will I know when I'm in labour?" she smiled and said: "Don't worry my dear, you'll know alright when your baby's coming!"

As I tried to settle down to sleep that night I knew that something was different but as I didn't have any pain I had no idea that I was about to go into labour. However, at about two o'clock, I woke up with an acute backache. I still didn't realise that this was the beginning of my labour as I was expecting to feel pain in my tummy and not my back! In my ignorance I lay there tossing and turning for several more hours until finally the pain became so acute that I had to wake my room-mate up and ask her to go and fetch the duty Sister. As I lay there alone in the cold little attic room, waiting for somebody to come and help me, I became very afraid. I suddenly began to worry that something could go wrong and my baby might die. The more I thought about this, the more distressed I became as I realised that even if the baby didn't die, I was still going to lose it. Whether I had a boy or a girl didn't really matter now; whatever it was, somebody out there was waiting to take it away from me forever.

Thinking about this now it occurred to me just how vulnerable we are when we are born and how dependant upon our mothers to love us. There's no guarantee that there will be loving arms to hold us and perhaps we'll be seen as just one more burden. Whether our parents are rich or poor is not really important; what matters is whether they welcome us. It is widely accepted now that deep and lasting hurts can be inflicted upon us in childhood, even whilst we are in the womb, and these wounds can affect the way we in turn relate to our own children. A vicious cycle can begin which may take generations to heal.

One thing we can be sure of is that God loves each little child that comes into the world; Psalm 139 tells us that He watched us taking shape in our mother's womb, an immensely comforting thought. However, such lofty thoughts were very far from my mind in those early morning hours as the pains increased. I became more and more distressed, not by the pain but by the horrible thought that my child might grow up believing that he or she was unloved and unwanted. Nothing could have been further from the truth. I so longed to keep this child and I yearned for a miracle to happen that would allow me to do so. But in the meantime the contractions were increasing and by the time help came, I was in considerable pain. I was relieved to see that it was Sr. Marie Jude who was on duty that night. I knew I was in good hands.

Sister assured me that I still had a few more hours before the baby would be born and after settling me down in the labour ward with one of the girls to keep an eye on me, she went off to attend to her other duties. I found it too uncomfortable to lie down, so with some difficulty I scrambled off the high labour bed and walked around the room. As I looked at the gleaming instruments in the glass cabinets I tried to imagine what they might be used for I had never heard of such things as forceps, which in retrospect is perhaps just as well; that would have been one more thing to worry about!

As I walked restlessly around the labour ward I was filled with fear; I didn't really know what to expect. In today's world such ignorance seems incredible. Sr. Marie Jude finally came back to check on me and after several more pain-filled hours, I gave birth on the 20th November, 1964 to a beautiful baby girl whom I named Kathryn. She was a lovely healthy baby and like every new mother I was smitten the moment I set eyes on her and I was sure that when my family saw her they would be so besotted with her too that they'd let me take her home. Surely nobody would take her away from me?

I enjoyed the first two weeks after Kathryn was born as I could spend a lot of time with her. I loved taking care of her and each morning I would carefully bathe and feed her before undertaking some light duties. We were discouraged from spending too much time with our babies, but who could resist cuddling such precious little bundles and only the hardest of hearts would try to stop us.

After about two weeks I had to start full-time work again and was assigned to cleaning the nuns' quarters which was not heavy work. Although we were not supposed to visit the nursery outside feeding and bath times, as soon as I had finished my duties I would hurry along to the nursery to spend as much time with my baby as possible. Picking her up when nobody was around, I would sing to her and tell her of the wonderful future we would have together.

"Don't worry," I said. "Nobody's going to take you away from me. We'll get a little flat and I'll take you to the park everyday; it will be wonderful, you'll see." Tears rolled down my cheeks as Kathryn looked up at me with her huge blue eyes. "Please God, please God!" I said desperately, "don't make me give her away." But the heavens were silent.

One day Sister Marie Jude came along and found me cradling Kathryn. "You're making it very hard on yourself, child. You know you have to give her up. Even now her adopters are getting ready to collect her." I felt utterly heartsick and helpless as I laid my precious baby down in her cot.

As the dreaded day grew nearer I feverishly devised plans in a last ditch attempt to keep my precious little baby. I had wild notions of running off with her and daydreamed of finding a live-in job in a hotel where I would somehow hide her in my room. I was becoming increasingly desperate.

Sister Marie Jude, who knew the turmoil I was going through, sent for me one day. "I know how hard this is for you Margaret." she said. "Why don't you ask God to help you make a decision?" "God?" I exclaimed angrily. "What does He care?"

"Well as a matter of fact He cares very much" she said quietly. "He loves you and your baby, and only wants what is best for you both." I found this very hard to swallow; I was full of bitterness and anger. Although I knew it was my own fault I was in this predicament, nevertheless I wanted to hit out at somebody, anybody, and God seemed to be the obvious target. Later that evening however, I thought about Sister Marie Jude's words and went to the empty chapel. As I knelt before the tabernacle, all the pain and fear of the past few months welled up and I cried out, "Oh God, please help me. Show me what to do." This was probably the first time I had prayed from the heart as opposed to merely 'saying prayers.' I felt rather foolish as I didn't really expect God to listen, much less do anything. I was still pretty sure He was angry with me, but I had nobody else to turn to.

We were allowed visitors at weekends and my oldest brother Alfie who had a car was a regular visitor. He brought my mother with him and we often went out for tea. We were not allowed to take the baby with us, of course, and I felt that already she was no longer mine. I was sure once my mother saw the baby she would relent and tell me to bring her home but although I could see she was very upset, she was adamant I would have to give her up for adoption. "I just couldn't cope with a baby Margaret. You would have to go out to work and leave her with me and I'm just not up to it" she told me sadly. I knew in my heart she was right.

The days sped by and Christmas was drawing near. I had spent my 18th birthday in an institution and now I was going to spend what should be the happiest time of the year there. I always loved Christmas and everything about it, but this year was the most miserable time of my life and nothing could change that.

"You're never out of that place. Are you turning into a religious maniac?" laughed one of the girls, as she spotted me coming out of the chapel yet again. I had not confided my secret prayers to anybody for fear of being ridiculed but each day I went into the chapel where I made the same desperate plea. "Please God help me to make the right decision." I was sure He would send in the cavalry at the last minute; surely they wouldn't make me give up my precious baby; it would be too cruel.

Christmas came and went but I couldn't muster much enthusiasm or goodwill. The adoptive parents were due to collect Kathryn soon and I have never spent a more wretched Christmas and New Year. After much agonising, and having explored every possibility, I knew I was beaten. I really had no alternative. I would have to give my baby up for adoption; hand her over to somebody who could give her security and the material things I couldn't provide. With a heavy heart I told Sister Marie Jude I had reached a decision.

"You are doing the right thing, child, I know it's the hardest thing you will ever have to do, but trust God. He'll take care of you and your baby." I didn't believe that for one minute. Why would God care about me? After all, I was a 'bad girl' wasn't I? I was getting the punishment I deserved and I would just have to learn to live with it. The trouble was, my baby was being punished too as she would never know me; never know how much I loved her and might grow up thinking she was just abandoned. This was the worst aspect of it, my utter powerlessness.

On that last morning I got up very early and took extra care bathing and dressing Kathryn. I carefully pinned a couple of religious medals to her vest. "Honestly, I really do love you. You will have a wonderful life I'm sure." Although we were given very little information about the adoptive parents, I had been told that Kathryn was being adopted by a farmer and his wife and I could only pray that they would love her.

"You are going to live on a farm and you will probably have a pony. I always dreamed of having a pony" I told her as she gazed solemnly at me. My tears spilled onto the new white shawl I had bought as a parting gift; not much to express my love for her, but the very best I could afford. I tried desperately to prolong those last moments before she was taken away. After all, I would never see her again. "Please forgive me" I sobbed as they came to collect her. "I love you with all my heart and I promise I will never forget you."

I wasn't allowed to see the adoptive parents and after handing my baby over to Sister Felicity, I fled to my room where I collapsed on my bed and wept bitterly. When I heard the sound of a car starting I ran to the window desperately trying to scribble down the registration number in the forlorn hope that somehow I would be able to trace the owners and thus, track down my child, but I didn't have a clue how to go about it. I had been watching too many movies! That little scrap of paper stayed with me for many years until somebody threw out the dilapidated suitcase it was hidden in.

The next six weeks passed in a haze of misery. I was dreading the next stage of the adoption. When my baby was three months old I would have to go to the Social Work department and sign the final papers. Legally up until the twelfth week after her birth, I had time to change my mind and the adopters would have had to return her to me. I realise now that they must have gone through agony too but at that stage I'm afraid all I could think about was how I felt. As I sat in the office with the adoption papers in front of me I was shaking like a leaf. Even the Social Worker was upset as she handed me the pen - we both knew I would never see my child again. As I walked out into the pouring rain, I swore that I would never be hurt like that again. Bitterness and anger formed a hard shell around my heart and I made an inner vow: "Nobody, but nobody is ever going to get near my heart ever again!"

CHAPTER FIVE

Out of the Frying Pan!..

In his heart a man plans his course,
but the Lord determines his steps.
(Proverbs 16: 9)

I worked for a while in a local carburetor factory in a mind-numbing job that a chimpanzee could just as easily have been trained to do. I didn't really care what I did: I felt so wretched and bereft. How had I managed to make such a mess of my life in the short time since I'd left school? What about all the predictions about the bright future that lay ahead of me? I wasn't so very bright after all, was I? And even if I was, what good had it done me? I was filled with self-loathing and bitter self-recrimination. My self-esteem had been low before I became pregnant and it was completely destroyed now. Only the fear of Hell stopped me from committing suicide. "Yeah, that would be just my luck. Make a mess of my life and then spend eternity in Hell!" I told myself bitterly.

The inner pain was indescribable and there was nobody I could confide in. I knew I'd have to get away from Barrow with its painful memories and in early spring headed off to work at a holiday camp in North Wales for the summer season. I tried to put the events of the past year behind me but it was impossible. Never a day went by without my thinking of my baby. How would I be able to live not knowing where she was; how could anybody love her as much as I did? Every time I saw a baby in a pram, I fled in tears. Out there somewhere was my precious little girl; but where was she? My drinking increased again as I tried desperately to dull the pain but no matter how much I drank, the pain was still there when I sobered up and I could see no way out. Going to work in a holiday camp was just one more attempt to escape my sorrow, but it would only lead to more problems.

"Are we mad or what?" I turned to my friends as the train pulled out of the station. We'd never worked away from home before and here we were, leaving everything behind to go and work in a holiday camp. After spending a cold and miserable night trying to sleep on the hard wooden benches of the waiting room in Crewe station, we eventually arrived at Pwllheli in North Wales, feeling tired and decidedly seedy. The heavens opened as we trudged through the gates.

"Whose bright idea was this?" I said as we found ourselves herded into a waiting area with about two hundred others. "Charming I must say!" said Audrey, one of my friends. "We've had nothing to eat since last night, haven't had a wash for twenty-four hours and now we've got to wait in this cattle market." Surely, things could only get better?

My visions of strutting around in a bright red jacket entertaining the holidaymakers with songs and witty repartee, bringing a little joy and sunshine into the lives of the weary masses quickly evaporated! As we sat there, steam rising from our wet clothes, I began to wonder if I had 'blown it' yet again; nothing seemed to work out as planned.

"You must be joking!" I said, "I don't want to do that." I had been offered a job as a chalet maid and certainly didn't relish the idea of cleaning up after drunken youths.

"It's only for a short time until we get you something better," said the recruiting officer smoothly. Having come all this way, I could hardly return home without having earned a penny. "Ok." I said reluctantly. Early next morning I reported for duty and was handed a large bunch of keys together with a trolley containing bucket, mop and a variety of cleaning materials. With the keys strung around my waist I felt like a gaoler and forty years ago, the chalets were in fact more like cells than holiday homes. "Huh!" I thought, "so much for a convent education!"

My time at Butlin's was interesting to say the least! I quickly made friends with some of the wilder people there. When I look back now, I can see that I spent a lot of time trying to escape emotional pain and pretending to be somebody I wasn't and Butlin's was certainly a good place to flee reality. After our days work, we were free to join the campers and had access to all the camp facilities. We were very poorly paid, however, and in order to finance our drinking sprees, most people took an additional evening job in one of the shops or bars. It was hard work and long hours and I have to smile when I hear people say; "What do you think this is then - a holiday camp?"

One day as I hurried round a corner I ran straight into somebody who looked familiar. I realised it was one of the Irish girls who had been in Brettargh Holt at the same time as me. However it was obvious I was just an embarrassment to her and as I opened my mouth to speak, she dashed off. I felt hurt as I had so many things I wanted to ask her but obviously I was just a painful reminder of that sad time in both of our lives. I realised that wherever I went, I would be faced with constant reminders of my baby and there was no way I could put it out my mind for very long. Holiday camps are family places and I was surrounded by happy families, often with babies about the same age as mine.

"Wake up, wake up!" I tried to stagger to my feet but it was hopeless. My friends were trying to sober me up and get me back to our chalet but I couldn't stand; I was too badly sun burnt. We had gone to the beach on our day off, taking bottles of cider and wine with us. The inevitable happened, I had too much to drink and fell fast asleep in the blazing sun. When I woke up I must have looked rather bizarre. My skin was burnt to a crisp and I was so stiff I could hardly walk. My friends put me on the miniature train packed full of gaping holiday-makers and took me to the first aid post, where I was given a severe ticking off, but I was too ill to care. The nurse issued me with a bottle of calamine lotion and a warning that I had three days to get better and resume my duties or I was "off the camp." There was no time for sentiment or sympathy; if you couldn't work then you were sent home.

Luckily for me, my chalet mate Margaret was a good friend and each day before she left for work, she applied the soothing lotion to my burnt limbs, coming home at lunchtime to check on me. "Don't worry" she said cheerily. "We'll soon have you back on your feet again – and back at the bar!" She knew me only too well. Sadly, I heard some years later that she had died from a drugs overdose. She was a kind generous person who had got into bad company and paid the ultimate price.

When the holiday season finished in September, I went to work in Brighton, taking a live-in job in a large hotel. It was a fun place to be in 1965 and for a small town girl like me I thought it was wonderful with its Bohemian atmosphere and quirky pubs. Each year on Bank Holidays, the Mods and Rockers roared into town on their motorbikes and scooters much to the dismay of the local residents and police force. The Mods with their parkas and long woolly scarves, favoured scooters, whilst the Rockers, dressed in black leather and filthy denims rode powerful motorbikes. Unfortunately, the rivalry which sprang up between the two groups became vicious at times and terrible fights broke out with people wielding broken bottles and chains as weapons: many people were seriously injured. Sometimes the atmosphere was positively evil and I did my best to avoid the seafront when the gangs were on the streets.

After about six months of hectic life in Brighton I was ready to move on again and in May 1966 I went back to work at Butlin's in North Wales. I'd had enough of cleaning out chalets, however, and this time I got a much nicer job, working in the nursery. I loved taking care of the babies and as I held one of them in my arms I could pretend for a moment it was my own child and that the whole sad episode had never happened. Never a day went by when I didn't think of my little girl, wondering where she was and scanning the faces of toddlers of the same age, desperately hoping that by some miracle she would appear and I would recognise her.

During this time I became very friendly with David, a tall handsome young Welshman who worked in one of the restaurants. He was kind and sympathetic when I told him about the baby and we soon began to go out together. He planned to leave the camp before the end of the season to work on a trawler sailing out of Lowestoft, and he asked me to join him in Suffolk. As it was almost the end of the season, I decided I had nothing to lose and so we left for East Anglia where I soon found a live-in job in a local hotel.

David enjoyed working on the trawler and was earning good money whilst I soon made new friends in the hotel. Hotel work, especially in those days when most staff lived in, is a little like living in a small village; a close camaraderie develops between staff working in such close proximity, especially as most of us were strangers to the area. We created our own entertainment, organising trips to the nearby town of Yarmouth on our days off or staff talent contests in the evenings. The food was excellent, the

company was great and life should have been good but
once again my loneliness and craving to be loved had got
me into trouble and I had only myself to blame.

It was a bright, sunny morning and people were going
about their business as usual in the bustling fishing port but
I felt miserable, apprehensive and sick with fear as I walked
into the doctor's surgery. The kindly old doctor looked up
from his notes saying, "Well, we have the results back and
it's positive. You are definitely pregnant, my dear." I don't
know why the doctor's words should have come as such
a shock but they did, and painful memories flooded back.
It was obvious to the doctor when he examined me that
this was not my first baby, and the whole sorry tale came
pouring out. He was very sympathetic and held my hand
until the tears subsided. Issuing me with a prescription
for iron tablets he assured me of his support which meant
a lot to me living in a strange town with no friends to turn
to. I was glad my family was far away; I felt deeply
ashamed of myself. "Don't worry my dear" he said. "I'm
sure everything will work out fine for you this time and
you will be able to keep this baby."

"Oh yes" I said. "There's no way I am giving this baby up;
even if I have to live in a tent. I couldn't go through that
again!" I was adamant; no matter what anybody said, I
would never be parted from this child.

"You idiot, will you never learn!" I berated myself bitterly.
Staring at the bottles of painkillers in the chemist's shop as
I waited for my iron tablets, the thought occurred to me that
a bottle of Scotch and a handful of pills would put an end to

my troubles. But if I did that, I would be taking an innocent life along with my own wretched one. "The baby doesn't deserve to die, even if I do," I thought bitterly.

"What's wrong with you, you fool?" I fought back the tears as I thought once again of how I'd messed up my life. I'd had a good education, the chance to go to university and do something worthwhile with my life and instead I just seemed to lurch from one crisis to another and it was my own fault. I was deeply unhappy but determined that I would try to be a good mother to this baby and I decided that no matter what David said, I was going to keep this baby. Perhaps I could get a live-in job in a hotel after it was born if David abandoned me.

But David was delighted. "That's wonderful news! I'm so pleased. We'll get married right away. You will marry me wont you?" said David rather anxiously. He must have sensed even then that I had reservations. I was relieved at his reaction but at the same time apprehensive: although he was very sweet and kind I wasn't really sure we would be compatible marriage partners. However I buried my misgivings, after all at least this time I could keep my baby and I knew that David who was a good and kind man, would be a good father.

After scraping together enough money to buy a cheap ring we made hasty arrangements for the wedding and were married on the 15th of August, 1966 in the local Catholic Church in Lowestoft. I had toyed with the idea of getting married in the Registry Office, telling myself that if it didn't work out, at least I wouldn't have been married in the eyes of the Catholic Church. But I soon realised this was totally hypocritical and unfair on David so I decided to get married in Church in the hope that somehow, if I made sacred vows, God would help me. After all, marriage was a sacrament; surely with God's help I could make it work? This was not the best basis for marriage but of course David was oblivious to what was going on in my head. The wedding was a rather forlorn affair, just the two of us and two witnesses who worked with me at the hotel. After the ceremony we made our way to a local Chinese restaurant where we had a rather subdued meal and the following day we left for Wales where we were to make our home with David's mother.

CHAPTER SIX

Vale of Tears

I lift up my eyes to the hills,
where does my help come from?
My help comes from the Lord
(Psalms 121: 1)

My first impression of South Wales was none too favourable. As I stepped onto the platform of the neglected little railway station at Merthyr Vale, the first thing I noticed was the litter and the small flock of sheep hurtling down the platform in a panic, desperate to escape the alighting passengers. "Oh, don't' worry" laughed David. "You'll soon get used to them." "I don't think I want to." I muttered under my breath. As an introduction to life in the valleys, it did not bode well.

The little villages of Merthyr Vale and Aberfan are not the prettiest of places and in those days were even more forlorn. At least the locals were friendly and went out of their way to welcome me. Separated by the River Taff which winds its way down to Cardiff, the villages were dominated by the large coal pit which in those days sat right in the centre. The coal mine was at the centre of village life and almost every household had at least one member of the family working underground. Moving in with your mother-in-law is not the ideal start to married life and what made it worse was the fact that I had never even met her, but David's mother Katie was very kind hearted and welcomed me into her home.

In order to qualify for maternity benefits it was important that I work for as long as possible and I soon found work in a factory on an industrial estate some miles away which meant I had to catch an early morning bus. Most of the passengers worked in the same large industrial estate and I quickly became one of the gang, enjoying the good natured banter each morning. Friday mornings were guaranteed to be especially lively as the workers were in a good mood, looking forward to having two days off and the talk usually centered on our plans for the weekend.

One particular Friday morning in October, it took twice as long to get to work due to an unusually heavy fog. The company on the bus was much quieter than usual and we were glad when we finally reached Treforest. That Friday turned out to be one of the most tragic and unforgettable days in the history of South Wales. There have been many accidents over the years in the coal pits and the locals were only too aware of the constant dangers of life underground, but the events that unfolded that day overshadowed anything that had gone before.

During the lunch break the factory radio was tuned in as usual to the latest pop music when suddenly the programme was interrupted by a news bulletin which silenced our sing-along. Apparently a coal tip in Aberfan had somehow shifted, engulfing the village school in tons of industrial waste and according to early reports the death toll was rising by the hour. We listened with mounting horror, hoping the reports were exaggerated: it couldn't be true. Those coal tips had been there for many years; they were part of the scenery, a kind of black Alps towering over the valley. Why would they suddenly move? We learned later that an underground stream had been relentlessly undermining the massive tip for many years until finally it collapsed, releasing a foul torrent of black slurry smothering everything in its path.

Above the village of Aberfan today, a new road cuts through the hills above the place where the school stood and there is nothing left of the sinister peaks which once towered over the valley. Even the colliery has disappeared; the site has been levelled off and all that remains is buried hundreds of feet beneath the grazing sheep. But on that dark morning of 22nd October 1966, the unthinkable happened.

Apart from the unusually heavy fog, it started out much like any other day as groups of chattering children made their way to Pantglas Primary School in Moy Road, Aberfan. At least it was Friday and they had the weekend to look forward to. Some of the children were planning to meet up at the local park on Saturday morning for a game of soccer whilst others were looking forward to a shopping trip to nearby Pontypridd or even Cardiff. However their plans

would never come to pass. Shortly after nine o'clock as
the last echoes of the school bell died away, a deadly
tide of black slurry moved silently and swiftly down the
mountainside, swallowing everything in its path, including
Pantglas Junior School. A total of one hundred and forty-
four people died in the Aberfan disaster; one hundred and
sixteen of them children, and five of their teachers perished
alongside them. Others were buried alive in their homes,
perhaps as they reached for their newspaper, enjoying the
first cup of tea of the day unaware of the silent killer
moving inexorably closer.

Those of us who lived in Aberfan or Merthyr Vale were
allowed home early from work that day and a special
bus came to collect us. The bus was eerily silent as we made
our way home, each wrapped in our own thoughts, not
knowing what to expect. It took three hours to make the
forty-five minute journey home as emergency vehicles
from all over South Wales raced to Aberfan. Only vehicles
carrying residents were allowed into the valley. Many of the
passengers on the bus were frantic with worry as they had
children or grandchildren who attended Pantglas School.
What were the thoughts that raced through their mind on
that interminable bus journey? Would they ever see them
again?

The sight that greeted us as the bus rounded the final bend
and dropped us at Merthyr Vale station was a nightmare
scenario. The first thing I noticed was that the black peaks
which sat atop the coal tip were no longer there. Dozens of
fire engines, ambulances and police vehicles crowded the
narrow streets as emergency service personnel from all over

South Wales scrambled to the scene. Helicopters hovered over the area like anxious flies and arc lights had been put in place in an effort to cut through the gloom. A pall of thick black coal dust hung in the air and the sound of wailing could be heard as parents gathered frantically outside of what remained of the little village school. The sight of family groups clinging desperately to each other, some of them mute with shock, others wailing pitifully will stay with me for the rest of my life. They were hoping against hope that rescuers might yet pull some survivors from the thick black mud. But it was a forlorn hope.

That night, teams of rescuers desperately searched for survivors, some of them frantically scrabbling with their bare hands, others using picks and shovels. It was too delicate an operation at this stage to use mechanical diggers; whilst there was still the slightest hope that somebody might be buried alive beneath the slurry; the rescuers had to use caution. People flocked in from all over the valleys just wanting to help in any way possible but as the hours passed it became increasingly unlikely that anybody would be pulled out alive. As the time passed, the bulldozers moved in to complete the grim task, the roar of their engines drowning out the grief stricken cries of relatives as yet another tiny victim covered in black sludge was carried off to the little chapel which served as a temporary mortuary. By night time as hopes had faded, the mood turned from sorrow to anger. As usual, God bore the brunt of the blame – even those who called themselves atheists blamed God!

As the bodies of the victims of that terrible disaster were

recovered one by one, the question hung in the air: "Why?" How could a loving God allow such a thing to happen? If that monstrous monument to industry had to move, why did it happen at 9.05 am just as the last child sat down in class? Why not 8.05 when the classrooms were empty? Why Friday, the last day of the school week and not Saturday when the school would have been closed for the weekend? There are no easy answers and few presumed to offer any.

However it was clearly men, not God, who piled industrial waste high above a school and chose to ignore warnings that such a disaster was possible due to the underground stream which flowed beneath the tip. Although nobody would admit it, greed and an unwillingness to cut profits was at the root of it and there was a groundswell of anger aimed at the National Coal Board. If only they had listened to the warnings of those who predicted that just such a disaster was possible but as is often the case, the cost of remedying the problem was considered to be too high. But nobody could put a price on the terrible loss of life and suffering that followed.

As it happens, it subsequently cost the government millions of pounds to clear the area and many other such sites throughout South Wales, but it was too late for the people of Aberfan and the village was left with scars which no amount of money could heal. Almost a whole generation had been wiped out and a residual bitterness remained in the village for many years.

Christmas that year was a cheerless event. Who could

celebrate in the midst of such tragedy? Valiant efforts were made for the sake of the surviving children but nobody's heart was really in it. The village could only wait for the findings of the official enquiry, but few believed that it would be anything more than a Public Relations exercise and the result would be a 'whitewash' of the whole tragic affair, with nobody taking responsibility for the consequences of negligence and greed.

The New Year arrived and the time soon came for me to stop work as I began to make preparations for the baby. This time it was different; nobody was going to take this child away from me and I eagerly awaited the birth. I really didn't mind whether I had a boy or a girl, just so long as it was healthy and I could keep it and take care of it myself.

On Friday 10th March 1967, I went into Merthyr Tydfil to do some shopping and attend my ante-natal exercise class. The baby was not due for another week but I had been experiencing some discomfort and I suspected that my waters had slowly been breaking since early morning. When I told the nurse she went into overdrive. "My, but you're a cool customer!" she laughed. "Let's get you over to the labour suite at once!" She sent for a wheelchair and rushed me to the adjacent maternity hospital. It didn't take so long this time and three hours later I gave birth to a beautiful baby boy whom we named Simon, and a happier phase of my life began.

As the summer approached, David and I both felt the old urge to move on. Having worked in North Wales for a couple of seasons, David was restless in his job on a building site. Obviously with the baby we could not go back to the holiday camp, but as we both loved North Wales David decided to apply for a job in a hotel in Abersoch, a popular resort on the Lleyn Peninsula. We managed to find a caravan to rent for the summer and David soon found work in a local hotel.

It was good to have a place of our own at last, even if was just a caravan and with the resilience of youth we managed to overlook the shortcomings. We had no electricity, just calor gas, and the gas mantles which had to be lit each night drove me to distraction. They were so fragile they disintegrated if the match touched them.

There was no mains water in the caravan and we had to walk across the field to a standpipe and fill large containers for all our needs. For holidaymakers who were only there for a week it was a novelty but with a small baby to look after it was quite hard work trying to do the weekly wash in a tiny sink and prepare meals on two burners! A trip to the bathroom meant walking across the fields in all weathers to the toilet block. But despite all this, it was our very first home and we were happy.

As we had no car, shopping trips meant pushing the pram two miles each way along a busy main road to the nearest supermarket where I loaded up with a week's supply of groceries. We had also adopted a beautiful Labrador dog. Trixie's owner had died suddenly and as there was nobody in the family able to take care of her, I volunteered. I have always loved dogs and so it was a joy for me to have this gentle addition to our family. Each day after I'd finished my chores I put Simon in his pram and headed off down to the beach with the dog where we spent many happy hours.

It was a magical summer but unfortunately as David's job was seasonal, we had to leave at the end of September. Once more we packed up our few belongings and headed off to look for work. This time we took the train north to Barrow where David was more likely to find a job.

Within a week of arriving, David found a job in the local paper mill and we managed to rent a small flat on the top floor of an old tenement building. These large old tenements had been built in the last century to house the thousands of workers who flocked to seek jobs in the burgeoning shipbuilding industry, as well as the busy iron and steelworks. This was a time when industry was thriving and Barrow was a boom town. From outside the old buildings looked rather shabby but inside the rooms were large and airy and with a lick of paint and some bright curtains, we soon managed to create a cosy little home. Although there was no bathroom and the toilet was outside on a draughty landing at least we had running water, even if it was cold and for us it was a step up from the caravan! We also had plenty of company at night as hordes of mice came into the flat from the old fashioned refuse chutes.

Although he worked very hard, David didn't earn much, and as I was too busy taking care of the baby to go out to work myself, money was tight but we were happy enough. We furnished the flat from second hand shops; we had no carpets, just rather worn linoleum but we were very proud of our little home. I kept it sparkling clean, scrubbing and polishing the lino and getting a first class shine on the shabby old furniture.

A trip to the shops meant bumping the pram down six flights of concrete steps, then walking back up to fetch Simon. It was much too dangerous to manoeuver pram and baby together down the worn, uneven stairs. The same exercise had to be carried out in reverse each time we got home. I had to take Simon upstairs, deposit him safely in his cot then go back down for the shopping. Then I had to make one more trip back down to haul the pram up the concrete steps. It was certainly good for my figure and I had no problems with my weight in those days!

After working in the paper mill for a year David was made redundant and decided to try his hand at something different. Although he had not had much education, David was bright and good at figures. He'd spotted an advertisement in the local paper placed by a large chain of newsagents who were recruiting managers. "Are you willing to give it a go?" he said. "I can't do this without your support." As the job description included provision of a modern flat, I thought we had nothing to lose so I encouraged him to apply for the job. We both had to attend the interview and it went well. Two days later we were offered the job and once more we were on the move.

CHAPTER SEVEN

Going up in the World!

A bruised reed He will not break
and a smouldering wick
He will not extinguish
(Isaiah 42: 3)

After a brief period of training, we were assigned to a newsagents shop in a pleasant suburb of Warrington. Set in the midst of a residential area, the shop was bright and modern and the flat above was luxurious compared to the places we had lived in so far. For the first time in more than two years of marriage we had a bathroom, instead of an outside toilet! We had lashings of hot water and central heating and Simon even had his own bedroom. The large airy lounge overlooked the village green and as I gazed out of the window, I felt very posh! "My, we've even got fitted carpets!" I thought proudly.

Although it was hard work as I had to help out in the shop as well as take care of a lively toddler, we enjoyed the challenge and life was good. Then things became a bit more difficult as just before Simon's second birthday I discovered that I was pregnant again. I wasn't sure how I would manage with a toddler, a new baby and a lively Labrador dog to cope with, as well as working in the shop. Somehow I didn't think it would work out and I suspected that our idyllic lifestyle would probably be short lived.

Each morning I would go down to the shop to help out during the busy period when people on their way to work popped in for a newspaper and packet of cigarettes. After that, the schoolchildren piled into the shop to stock up on sweets and fizzy drinks. One morning it was particularly hectic as Simon caused havoc in the shop whilst I was doing my best to keep an eye on him and serve customers at the same time.

"Look out missus!" one of the children shouted as I heard a sound like marbles rolling across the shop floor. "Your kid's emptied a box of aniseed balls all over the floor!" The children thought it was hilarious and highly entertaining but for me it was a nightmare.

"You should see what your dog's eating out there" said another. Whilst I was trying to sweep up the aniseed balls, our dog Trixie was enjoying a huge bar of chocolate on the grass outside the shop. Meanwhile Simon was distributing largesse in the form of chewing gum, chocolate bars and fruit drops to the local schoolchildren who were crowding the shop on their way to school. It was like some manic game show as the children tried to grab as many sweets as they could in the shortest possible time and I was exasperated. David had gone to the wholesalers and I was alone in the shop trying to keep things in order and supervise Simon at the same time. Just then the stock takers walked in; it was the last straw.

Although the accommodation was good, the wages were poor for the amount of responsibility we had and with another baby on the way it would be impossible for me to help David run the shop, so once more we loaded up a van and headed back to Barrow.

The baby was due in November but in the middle of September I went into premature labour and was rushed to hospital where I gave birth to a beautiful little girl whom we named Sara. Because she was born seven weeks early and weighed just 3lb 10 oz, she had to spend seven weeks in hospital and it was a very anxious time. I hated going home without her: it brought back too many painful memories.

Winter set in and with the daily visits to hospital in the bitter cold, I soon became ill with pleurisy. It was so frustrating being unable to visit Sara and I had to rely on David to relay reports of her progress. How I longed to hold her but I was ill for weeks and had to just pray that she'd pull through. Simon proudly announced to all and sundry that he had a baby sister but she was in a little greenhouse – his description of the incubator. Sara was finally allowed home in January 1970 and thankfully this coincided with our being allocated a council house where we stayed for almost two years until we'd saved enough to buy a little terraced house of our own.

David started work in the local shipyard and life was good. Money was still tight now that we had a mortgage, but I always managed to find enough money to buy a couple of bottles of cider and beer at the weekends. I was now drinking at home. What had started out as a solution to a babysitting problem became a way of life for me and unwittingly what had seemed like a good idea became a nightmare.

David was a talented snooker player and was on the team at a local social club. He was also a keen card player and as we couldn't easily find a babysitter, David solved the problem by buying in some beers for me one weekend so that I could have a drink whilst he was at the club. That was how I began to drink at home; it was as simple as that. I suspect David saw it as a way of keeping me quiet too; if I was enjoying a drink at home I was less likely to complain about his regular nights out with the boys.

The drinking was also a way of drowning the turmoil I felt inside. There was an indescribable restlessness within me; a deep sense of isolation and loneliness. David was a kind and generous man; I had two lovely children a decent home and yet I was deeply unhappy. I discovered that drink numbed the pain for a while at least. My motto became: "When I drink, I don't have to think!" Once the children were settled down for the night I started drinking.

"Hurry up, we'll be late for church!" Sunday mornings were a hassle, because despite having a bad hangover from the previous night's drinking, I made a point of going to Mass each week. I can't say that it meant much to me at this point, it was more a matter of habit with a bit of fear thrown in. I had a strong sense of duty and I felt I was already in God's bad books so I didn't want to antagonise Him further! I knew that I was drinking too much and this filled me with shame, but I couldn't stop and I despised myself for this. I berated myself for my weakness and going to Mass didn't really help because I just felt even guiltier.

By now I was experiencing panic attacks, especially in confined spaces and often during Mass I had to fight off the urge to run out of the church. But perhaps God would punish me even more if I stopped going to church? The distorted image I had of God had been carried over from my childhood and I still thought of Him as a harsh vengeful judge who despised weakness. I felt that I had to go to church at least once a week to appease Him. Sadly, my faith had not progressed from that of a frightened seven year old child.

I remembered the eve of my seventh birthday; our teachers had told us that once we reached the age of seven we would be held responsible for our actions and if we committed a mortal sin and died before we had a chance to go to confession, we would spend eternity in hell! I didn't know what eternity meant but I'd heard enough descriptions of the torments of hell to know that whatever it meant, I didn't want to go there! I dreaded my seventh birthday and I was fearful all that day that I might somehow commit a 'mortal sin' and be consigned to everlasting flames should I die during the night.

By the age of seven, I'd experienced the sudden deaths of people I loved and knew only too well that there was a distinct possibility that I might go to bed one night and not wake up just like Aunty Bell had. This is the ugly face of religion and it's no wonder that people are turned off by such a false picture of God. I believed that getting to heaven depended entirely on how we behaved and had no real understanding of salvation. I thought that 'good' people went to heaven and 'bad' people went to hell. It was as simple as that and I certainly didn't consider myself a 'good' person; I was far too weak and I was sure that when I died I would be cast into Hell.

At the weekends I felt jittery and shaky. "I think it's the booze." My sister Sheila looked at my shaking hands. "You drink far too much, Margaret, and that can give you the shakes in the mornings. You are like Jekyll and Hyde. Once you start drinking you become a different person." I was angry that she dared to suggest that alcohol had anything to do with my problems and became very defensive. "Don't be stupid! It's got nothing to do with drink. It's my nerves." Somehow it was more acceptable to have 'bad nerves' than be a problem drinker.

If anybody had mentioned the word alcoholic I would have been furious. The word gave me the shivers and I was determined to find some other reason for feeling so terrible. Most alcoholics are in denial and blame everything and everybody for their drinking and I was no exception.

"If we didn't live here things would be different" I told myself. "If I had a job I wouldn't drink. I only do it because I'm bored." When David suggested yet another move, this time back to South Wales I readily agreed. We rented out our house in Barrow and moved back in with my mother-in-law in Merthyr Vale until we found our own place. I was on the run again.

I knew by now that I had problems but didn't really associate them with my heavy drinking. I thought that I drank because I had problems and was sure that if I could find the right job things would be different and I wouldn't need to drink. I decided that I'd had enough of dead end jobs such as factory and shop work so I enrolled on a shorthand and typing course at the local college as part of a Government re-training scheme. It meant that I got a small allowance each week whilst I was learning.

I soon picked up shorthand and typing skills and enjoyed the company of the other women on the course, especially the evenings after college when we went to the local pub. These friends drank much too slowly for me and a couple of drinks lasted them all evening. I was too embarrassed to let them see how much I was actually drinking so on the pretext of going to the ladies, I sneaked into the other bar where I downed a couple of whiskies.

"You can't handle it can you? Doesn't take much to get you drunk does it?" These were some of the comments my friends made as my speech became more and more slurred. In fact I'd had three or four drinks to their one and they couldn't understand why I seemed to be so quickly affected by one glass of wine! Sneaking extra drinks is typical alcoholic behaviour as we try desperately to hide the true extent of our drinking.

On other occasions when David and I went out for the evening, I was so desperate for a drink at times that I would even finish off the dregs left in other people's glasses. When the pub stopped serving for the night I would panic. On the pretext of going to the toilet I looked around the tables and when nobody was looking I would quickly finish off any drinks I saw lying around. Although I felt ashamed of myself, the need for a drink overcame any embarrassment.

Every Monday morning was the same; I felt dreadful, my hands were shaking and I looked terrible. Through sheer willpower and determination I made it into college where I struggled to concentrate on the lectures. I had reached the stage where I needed a drink in the mornings but I was determined not to as I suspected that alcoholics drank in the mornings and to prove that I was not one, I gritted my teeth and took pills instead. To counteract the shakes I took tranquillisers during the day and sleeping pills at night. I was just exchanging one form of dependency for another.

Like most alcoholics I was stubborn and strong-willed and I made up my mind that I would pass the College exams if it was the last thing I did. "I'll show them!" I vowed. "I'm not an alcoholic; I'm just under a lot of pressure. So what if I have a few drinks to unwind at the weekend?" I was still in denial and determined to prove that I was in control.

In fact I managed to pass all the exams with flying colours and soon got a good job in the local Magistrates Clerk's Office. One of my duties was to take shorthand notes during the court cases which was interesting and enjoyable work. I should have been happy but I wasn't. I had one less excuse for drinking but that didn't stop me getting hopelessly drunk every weekend. I didn't realise it then but it was my inner emptiness that drove me to drink, not my outward circumstances and until I faced up to that, things could only get worse.

CHAPTER EIGHT

A Downward Spiral

The Lord upholds all those who fall
and lifts up all who are bowed down.
(Psalms 145: 14)

By now David had started to comment on the amount I was drinking and even accused me of being an alcoholic. This infuriated me and to prove to myself he was wrong I decided not to have a drink for two weeks, telling myself that an alcoholic couldn't possibly go for so long without a drink. As soon as the two weeks were up however I got very drunk to celebrate the fact I wasn't an alcoholic! I was in denial in a big way.

Although the children were not neglected physically and I tried to be a good mother, inevitably my drinking affected them. As soon as they were in bed I would get out the bottle and as David worked shifts at a local factory, I was often alone. I became so paranoid that when Simon came downstairs at night for a drink of water, I accused him of spying on me and reporting back to his Dad. This must have been bewildering for an eight year old to deal with.

By this stage of my drinking I had started hiding bottles of alcohol in various places around the house and sometimes I forgot where I'd hidden them. I ransacked the house becoming more and more desperate in my search for the bottles. One night I discovered some bottles of beer in the freezer and as I was desperate for a drink, I put them under the hot water to speed up the process of defrosting. Of course the bottles shattered and I was heartbroken as I watched my precious booze gather in a puddle amid the broken glass. I think it was at this point that I first admitted to myself that this was not normal behaviour.

Shortly after this, I saw the film: 'The Days of Wine and Roses' on television and was absolutely horrified. The film tells the story of a couple who are alcoholics and one chilling scene depicts the husband desperately searching for a bottle of Scotch he has hidden in a greenhouse. The problem is it's a large commercial greenhouse and he can't remember which row he hid the bottle in. Growing increasingly desperate, he wrecks the greenhouse in a frantic search for his booze. This scene really hit home and I found that I could identify with the character's desperation. This shocked me to the core and that night I went to bed feeling more afraid than usual. I was sure I was going mad but I didn't know where to turn for help. Shame and fear prevented me from admitting that I needed help. I kept thinking about the film over the next few days but in order to drown out the reality of what was going on in my life I simply drank more and more.

Another wake-up call came when I walked the dog in the field behind our house and spotted a small mountain of empty Newcastle Brown bottles just opposite our back gate. I was indignant that somebody had littered the field like that until on closer inspection, I realised they were in fact my own empty bottles, Newcastle Brown being my preferred tipple at that time! Because I was ashamed of my drinking, I was paranoid and didn't want the neighbours to hear the rattle of my empties in the dustbin. I found what I thought was the perfect solution. I would stand on my rear doorstep and hurl the empty bottles over the wall into the adjacent field! But I was horrified when I saw just how many there were. I later discovered that disposing of empties is a common problem with alcoholics and people go to great lengths to disguise the rattle of the empties such as carefully wrapping them up in newspaper before placing them in the dustbin.

Although I didn't realise it at the time, I had also begun to hallucinate and on one occasion was convinced that a giant seagull was perched on the dressing table, biding its time before it attacked me. It was so real that I hastily pulled the bedcovers over my head in order to escape its malevolent gaze. Time was running out; how much longer could I continue to live in denial as my life spiraled dangerously out of control?

"Oh God if you're there please help me!" I rolled out of bed with a monumental hangover. Catching sight of myself in the mirror, I shuddered: "What a wreck! What's happening to me?" I was twenty-nine years old and looked more like forty-nine with my bleary bloodshot eyes and muddy complexion. Drink was affecting my health and my appearance. I weighed a little over seven stone and I looked dreadful. Every bone in my body ached, my tongue felt like sandpaper and I had a raging thirst. In addition, I was addicted to nicotine and smoked at least twenty cigarettes a day.

"That's it. I can't take any more. I swear I'll never drink again, but please God help me!" I lit up a cigarette and stared at my reflection. "If you help me God, I promise I'll try to be good." I bargained pathetically with God in sheer desperation. I knew that I couldn't carry on like this much longer.

I was certain by now that I was mad and would end up locked away in a mental hospital. I had a horror of mental illness and was sure that one day I would be committed to a locked ward. Although there was no denying there was something radically wrong with me, I still didn't realise I was an alcoholic. I had the classic image in my mind of an alcoholic. As far as I was concerned, an alcoholic was a homeless down and out, somebody who wandered the streets dishevelled and scruffy, swigging from a bottle and sleeping rough. I managed to kid myself that I was not that bad. After all I had a home and family as well as a responsible job. The shake in my hands I put down to 'nerves.' "I'm highly strung, that's all."

It was early January 1976, I had drank a lot at Christmas –

alcoholics love Christmas as it's a time of year when you can get away with excessive drinking; everybody's doing it. On New Years Day, 1976, I made a resolution. I would definitely do something about my drinking; I knew I couldn't carry on like this for much longer. But I was determined that I would beat this thing myself. I was far too proud to seek help and I was sure that with enough willpower I could solve my own problems.

I tried various ways to control my drinking such as drinking only beer or cider and not spirits. That didn't work; I still got drunk and felt awful. Next, I tried to control the number of drinks I had, limiting myself to drinking only at weekends. That too was a miserable failure because the 'weekends' became longer and longer, starting on Thursday and finishing on Monday! It seemed that once I took one drink I lost control and simply couldn't stop even though I intended to stick to just one or two drinks. Each time I woke up with a hangover I promised myself that this was definitely the 'last time.' After many futile attempts to control or stop drinking, I finally admitted defeat. It seemed that I couldn't live with drink but I couldn't live without it, so I felt there was only one solution – and I began to make plans to commit suicide.

David worked night shifts in a local factory and I decided that Friday night would be the best time to do it, after he'd left for work. I had a bottle of whisky and about a hundred sleeping pills stashed away. I decided that I'd take this lethal cocktail once the children were asleep as I didn't want them to find me dead. David would find me when he got home on Saturday morning; he wouldn't be home until about seven-thirty and by then it would be too late, I would have been dead for hours. This was definitely not a 'cry for help'; I meant business. A strange calm descended on me that week. I was convinced that if I was dead it would be better for my family. I was such a hopelessly weak wretch, they would all be better off without me. At last they would have peace.

After he'd finished his shift David always bought a daily paper at the factory gates. That particular Friday morning when went to buy his paper, he discovered his regular newspaper was on strike so he had to buy a different one. I went out to work as usual, conscious that this would be my last day at the office. On Monday no doubt the talk at the office would be focused on my sudden death. I could just imagine my colleagues saying things like: "Well, Margaret was the last person I would have thought would kill herself!" "Yes, she was always such a good laugh!" Like many alcoholics, I was a good actress and managed to hide the reality of what was going on in my life. I wore a mask, just as I had since my early teens. Nobody, not even David really knew how I felt.

On the Friday that I'd decided to commit suicide, I came home from the office at lunchtime and noticed that David hadn't bought his usual paper. As I idly turned the pages, a particular article caught my eye. It was headed: 'My Battle with the Bottle,' and was written by a recovering alcoholic. I became deeply engrossed in the story.

I was astonished: here was somebody describing exactly how I felt. I identified strongly with everything the writer said. He told of frequent 'geographical changes' when he'd moved from place to place in the vain hope that if he changed his surroundings the problem drinking would cease. How many times had I tried to do exactly the same in the belief that I only drank because I had problems? The truth slowly dawned on me. Maybe I had it the wrong way round: perhaps I had problems because I drank?

On the surface I had little in common with the man telling his story. He was a titled man who'd lived a privileged life; his 'geographical changes' had taken him to Antigua, the Bahamas and other exotic locations whilst mine had only led me up and down the M6! But when he described his guilt and shame and how he felt isolated and different from other people, I identified with him completely.

Despite his wealth and jet set lifestyle he had felt lonely and alienated. Finally admitting he couldn't quit drinking despite his best intentions, he decided suicide was his only option. He made up his mind to shoot himself and one night in a drunken stupor he told the barman in the local pub what he was planning. The barman just happened to be a recovering alcoholic himself and a member of Alcoholics Anonymous. He persuaded the suicidal customer that there was hope and begged him to at least give Alcoholics Anonymous a try before blowing his brains out!

After attending several meetings he managed to stop drinking and get his life back on track. Although it was not easy, with the help and support of others who had suffered from the same problem, he had not only quit drinking but found a new way of living. No longer using alcohol as a means of escaping reality, he learned how to face life and cope without the aid of drink.

After reading this man's story, I felt a ray of hope for the first time in years. It was a relief to discover that I was not alone and there were others who had the same problem and had managed to overcome it. Perhaps there was a chance for me after all? I decided to contact AA (Alcoholics Anonymous) as soon as possible.

That night when the children were asleep and David had left for work, I eyed the bottle of Scotch and the sleeping pills. I broke into a sweat as I tried to pluck up the courage to phone The Samaritans as I didn't know how to get in touch with AA. Finally, with shaking hands, I dialled the number and waited nervously for somebody to pick up the phone. I didn't have long to wait and before long I poured out my sorry tale to a kindly volunteer who listened to my tale of woe and promised to put me in touch with an AA member as soon as possible.

"Just stay where you are Margaret and I'll get somebody to call you who will be able to help you. And listen, your problem is more common than you think. I'm sure that AA will soon have you on your feet again!" I hoped he was right as I waited for the phone to ring.

I couldn't sit still and as I paced the room I glanced longingly at the bottle of whisky which seemed to beckon me. I was sweating profusely; I didn't want to drink, but the urge was strong and I knew that unless the person from AA rang soon, I wouldn't be able to hold out much longer.

I was startled when the phone rang and even more so when the caller introduced himself.

"Hello there, is that Margaret?" He had a strong Irish accent. "I'm Father John and I'm an alcoholic." I was stunned. Firstly I was surprised that the caller was a priest and secondly that he just admitted to a complete stranger that he was an alcoholic. I don't know why, but I certainly didn't expect a priest to be an alcoholic. I soon discovered that alcoholism is no respecter of persons and in AA I met people from all professions and walks of life.

Father John listened quietly while I poured out my tale of woe, before sharing a little of his own story with me. He had sunk pretty low because of his drinking and at one point slept rough on a beach in Cork. His superiors had branded him a hopeless case and packed him off to an institution: at least if they couldn't cure him they could control him. It was a damage limitation exercise at best and the authorities didn't expect him to survive. In the mental hospital however, he faced up to the fact that he was on the road to insanity and out of sheer desperation began to attend AA meetings.

"Remember Margaret, alcoholism is a sickness not a sin. When you stop drinking, you will find so many things will fall into place for you and life will start to get better. It's not easy, but you'll be surrounded by people who understand what you're going through. For us, one drink is too many and a hundred's not enough! The people at the meetings won't judge you or condemn you because they've been there too."

"But what will I do at Christmas time?" I lamented. "How will I cope without a drink?" Father John chuckled, "That's rather a long way off Margaret isn't it? It's only January now! Look, don't worry about the future; in AA we have a saying: "If you don't take the first drink, you won't get drunk. We just try to stay sober one day at a time. You know when you think about it, the fact is, today is all we have."

"What do you mean?" I asked. "Well Margaret, yesterday is gone forever and tomorrow might never come! So why waste time worrying about what's already past or what might never happen!"

Despite the fact that he was a priest, he never mentioned God or religion during that first conversation. It was only as I got to know him that we began to talk about these things. I told him that I believed in God but I wasn't sure that God believed in me! "Oh you'd be surprised" he laughed "Sure God has some very odd friends!" At least he had a sense of humour and I knew instinctively that he and I would get on well.

The nearest AA meeting at that time was twenty miles away in Cardiff and Father John promised to pick me up and take me to a meeting. This would mean a round trip of eighty miles twice a week on top of his parish duties and I was touched by such kindness from a total stranger. I was still cynical and suspicious and believed that people only helped you if there was something in it for them. It was my first encounter with the genuine concern for others that exists in the fellowship of Alcoholics Anonymous.

When I went to my first AA meeting it was like coming home and I felt an enormous sense of belonging. I found that people were warm-hearted and non-judgmental and I had an instant rapport with them. I had never experienced such compassion from complete strangers. Nobody questioned me or condemned me and my carefully built defenses quickly crumbled. I felt welcomed and accepted and after listening to their stories I was hopeful that if it worked for them, it could work for me too. It sounded a bit too simple but they assured me that the only way to stop drinking and stay sober was to stay away from the first drink. Although many of the stories were sad, there was lots of laughter at the meetings and I heard it said many times: "Take your sobriety seriously but don't take yourself too seriously!"

Nobody said to me "You are an alcoholic." This is something each person has to decide for themselves. But after listening to different stories, I identified with what I heard and I had no doubt that this was my problem too. These people had something that I wanted and I was willing to listen to them to hear how I could leave the misery behind and get back on track.

"Yes, it's simple Margaret. But it's not easy! If you don't take the first drink you won't get drunk. There's nobody who's too stupid to get sober, but there are lots who think they are too clever!"

The A.A. philosophy of taking life just one day at a time makes a lot of sense whether you are an alcoholic or not. I learned that the programme of recovery, whilst not being overtly 'religious', is spiritual. It is based on surrendering one's life and will to God, as you understand Him. Most of us had made a terrible mess of our lives when we were in control. What did we have to lose in handing over control to God?

Some people chose to call God a 'Higher Power' and it worked for them. Others who were antagonistic to religion, perhaps due to bad experiences they'd had when they were young, soon relaxed when they realised that AA is not allied with any denomination or creed and nobody tries to force any beliefs on to others.

Recovery in AA is based on a Twelve Step Programme, and Step One states: 'We admitted we were powerless over alcohol and that our lives had become unmanageable.' I had reached that point and I was ready to try anything that might restore me to sanity. If it had worked for all these people maybe it would work for me.

Alcoholism affects people from all walks of life and is no respecter of persons. It has nothing to do with intelligence, moral integrity or social standing and there were people from all walks of life at the meetings. In our group alone there was a barrister; shop assistants; a neurosurgeon; a monk; a priest and factory workers, as well as a titled lady, housewives, schoolteachers and a famous Hollywood actor who came to the meetings when he was visiting his family in Wales. People are treated as equals and we leave our professional standing, or lack of it, outside the AA meeting. I recovered from the physical effects of drinking fairly quickly, although I did initially suffer some very nasty withdrawal symptoms such as shaking and sweating for several weeks. In some of the early meetings I had to sit on my hands to stop them shaking and even holding a cup of tea without spilling it was difficult. Some days I felt I wouldn't make it through the day without a drink so it was suggested that I try to do it just an hour at a time. I did 'cold turkey' and came off the booze without the aid of any drugs. I was afraid that if I took tranquillisers I might just substitute one addiction for another.

Some nights I would pace the floor like a caged animal, I couldn't relax until the pubs were closed for the night and I knew I couldn't get hold of any alcohol. Twenty-four hour opening hours must make it more difficult for anybody who's trying to quit drinking and I'm glad it was unheard of when I was trying to stop. I would finally fall into bed in a state of exhaustion only to toss and turn most of the night. I frequently dreamt that I'd taken a drink and when I woke up and realised it was only water in the glass by my bed, it was a huge relief.

I hadn't realised just how sick I was, minimising the extent of my drinking. I told myself there were people who drank far more than I did and were worse than me. However when I began to listen to other people's stories in the A.A. meetings I discovered that what I had thought were nightmares, were in fact DT's - delirium tremens. On many occasions after a drinking session, I woke to see what I thought were hordes of rats swarming up the bed towards me. It was always the same - the rats would be within an inch of my face then suddenly disappear. And I remembered the incident of the imaginary seagull perched on my dressing table.

I had also suffered from alcoholic black-outs, whole periods of time that I simply couldn't account for. I would remember where I had been up to a certain point in the evening then after that it was a total blank; anything could have happened. Simon recently reminded me of an incident which I had completely forgotten. When we lived in Barrow, I had taken the children across to Piel Island on the little ferry that plied back and forth between the island and the mainland. It was a short crossing and a local boatman took passengers over to the island where you could spend a day wandering around the ruined castle or picnicking on the beach. There was also a pub on the island and this particular day I'd taken the children in with me whilst I had a few drinks. Of course the inevitable happened and we missed the last ferry. I had to go around the men in the pub begging for a lift back to the mainland. Fortunately, one of them took pity on us and we piled into his little boat. I had forgotten about this incident and no doubt Simon could tell many more such tales of my irresponsible behaviour when I drank. It was frightening to look back over those times and I was grateful that I got to AA before something really terrible happened.

As the days became weeks and the weeks became months, I began to recover and slowly regained a modicum of self respect.

"Your mother would be proud of you if she could see you. You're doing well Margaret. Keep it up!" said David. But unfortunately, it was too late for my mother to see me now. One day about a year ago when we were living with my mother-in-law, there was an urgent knocking at the door.

It was the owner of the local pub and I could tell by his expression something was horribly wrong.

"Can you come over and take a phone call? It's your sister. She said it's urgent." We didn't have a telephone and the only way my family could contact me in an emergency was to phone the pub across the road. The news was the worst possible; my dear mother had committed suicide that day and they had just recovered her body from the sea. It was a freezing cold day in January and I couldn't bear to think about my poor mother walking into the cold Irish Sea. It was just too horrible. I didn't sleep that night as images of my mother flashed before me. She must have been in a terrible state of mind.

The following day David hired a car and we made the sad trip north. It was a nightmare journey and I was in a state of turmoil as we covered the miles as fast as possible. I stared out at the snow covered fields in a haze of misery. What had happened? Why had my mother killed herself?

When we arrived we heard the sad details. My mother had been in a lot of pain and was convinced she had cancer. She was also being treated for acute depression. Mum lived with my sister and her husband who had welcomed her into their home and done their very best for her but the depression had taken a hold and life had obviously become unbearable. One day when she was alone, she'd simply put on her best clothes, took a bus to the beach and walked into the sea. I will never understand why she did that as I remember many years ago when a local child had accidentally drowned my mother had said: "I can't think of a more horrible way to die than drowning".

I was sorry that my mother wasn't around to see me now that I'd stopped drinking, especially as the last time I'd seen her was when I'd travelled to Barrow at New Year and I was too busy going out partying to even spend New Year's Eve with her and instead I had left her all alone. I felt deeply ashamed, but there was nothing I could do to change the past. I could only hope she was able to see me now and know that I was trying hard to change.

In the past the church took the view that suicide was an unforgivable sin, and refused to bury the victims in hallowed ground. This was a harsh judgement and there is certainly no scriptural basis for it. When I discussed my mother's death with my parish priest he asked me a question: "Margaret, how do you react when you hear that somebody has taken their own life?" I didn't need to think about it. "I feel sorry for them of course! People must be in a desperate state of mind to do that."

"Exactly!" Father Joe smiled. "And if we feel compassion for those who take their own lives, we can be sure that God has pity on them too. After all, only He knows the depth of their suffering and the anguish which overwhelmed them. Don't worry, Margaret, I'm sure your poor mother is with the Lord now." Despite his kind words the wounds of suicide in a family are devastating and there is a residue of guilt which remains for many years. You don't 'get over it,' you just learn to live with it.

After I had been sober for about six months we moved back

to Barrow and into our old home again and David and I both found jobs. I was deeply sad at the loss of my mother and the tragic circumstances surrounding her death and I was also deeply unhappy in my marriage. Now that I was no longer drowning my sorrows with alcohol, I had to face up to the fact that David and I were incompatible. The feelings I'd had before our wedding came back to haunt me and I knew I'd married David for the wrong reasons. If I had not been pregnant I would not have married him.

"David" I said one night, "this is just not working. Surely you must know that too?" I tried desperately to share honestly how I felt without in any way blaming him but he refused to admit that there was anything wrong with our marriage. "It's all in your mind!" he shouted angrily. "There's nothing wrong with our marriage – your problem is you read too many magazines!" and he stormed off to the club to play snooker.

I didn't know what to do. I spent hours walking on the beach turning the problem over and over in my mind but I could see no way out. If David wouldn't even admit we had problems then how could we sort things out?

The sea spray mingled with my tears as I walked for mile after lonely mile along the beach. I gazed out to sea, remembering my poor mother; I wished she was here now. "Please God, make me love David." My desperate prayer was lost on the wind and the only sound was the plaintive cry of a gull. I believed that marriage should be for life and I had tried hard for the past ten years to make it work but once I stopped drinking it became more difficult as I could no longer seek oblivion in a bottle. I was forced to face the painful truth. If I didn't do something soon, I was in danger of relapsing back into alcoholism but I could see no way out of my dilemma.

CHAPTER NINE

You Take the High Road...

Yet the Lord longs to be gracious to you;
He rises to show you compassion
(Isaiah 30: 18)

One of the Twelve Steps of Recovery in Alcoholics Anonymous suggests that we take a 'searching and fearless moral inventory of ourselves'. We are encouraged to face up to our personal shortcomings and it was painful at times. Getting sober and staying sober demands rigorous honesty and it's a well known fact that those who fail to stay sober generally lack the capacity to be honest with themselves. Chapter Five of the book 'Alcoholics Anonymous' opens with this statement:

"Rarely have we seen a person fail who has thoroughly followed our path. Those who do not recover are people who cannot or will not give themselves to this simple programme, usually they are men and women who are constitutionally incapable of being honest with themselves."

So if I was to stay sober it was obvious that I was going to have to face some hard truths. I knew that I was living a lie and that my marriage was a sham but I could see no way out. "Oh God, what am I going to do?" I cried out in desperation, but the heavens remained silent.

Another two years passed and I became more and more desperate, trying to hide things from the children and pretending that everything was fine. I felt that I was a miserable failure who had messed up my own and other people's lives and I deserved to suffer for the rest of my life.

"Come on, Margaret, you may as well enjoy yourself for once; there's room for one more," enthused my friend Joan. "Somebody cancelled at the last minute so why don't you join us?" Joan was trying to persuade me to join a group of friends who were travelling to Scotland for the weekend. They were going to the annual 'Bluebonnets Gathering' in Dumfries and there was a place going spare.

The Blue Bonnets Gathering is a hugely popular event when thousands of recovering alcoholics flock into the small Scottish town to celebrate their sobriety. The whole weekend was given over to listening to various speakers from home and abroad as well as social gatherings each evening. Although I had heard it was a wonderful weekend, I had no heart for anything. But my friend Joan was not one to give up easily.

"You look like you could use a break," she continued. "I don't know what's wrong with you lately; you're not exactly a bundle of laughs!"

I had shared many things with my friend Joan who had also had a hard time with alcohol, having been hospitalised several times. She was a good friend to me but I had not been able to share the reason for my unhappiness with her. To me, divorce was anathema and I already felt I was a failure: I didn't want to admit that my marriage was a farce too. I was deeply ashamed of feeling like this. David was a good man, why oh why didn't I love him? It was not his fault, it was just that we were incompatible. If only Joan knew how wretched I felt I knew she'd be shocked. I didn't want to drink again but the old notions about committing suicide had been tempting me lately and I couldn't admit this to anyone.

"Okay, why not? I'll come with you." I finally agreed. I couldn't muster much enthusiasm but at least it would get me away from home for the weekend. "The break will do you good," David said. Although he wasn't willing to face up to the truth about our marriage, he knew how unhappy I was.

The weather was glorious that weekend and my spirits lifted as we headed across the border into Scotland towards the little market town of Dumfries. There was a group of AA members from Aberdeen staying at our guesthouse and they were a friendly bunch.

"Hi! I'm Warren. Welcome to Scotland!" The owner of the deep, rich voice shook my hand and offered to fetch me a cup of tea. Already he had got off to a good start!

Warren was with the group from Aberdeen and we hit it off immediately. We spent that first evening swapping tales of the scrapes and embarrassing situations our drinking had got us into. The AA meetings were held in a large community hall and after the meeting there was a dance. It has to be seen to be believed just how much fun we 'ex-drunks' have when we get together in a gathering like that. And all stone cold sober!

The next morning was taken up with AA meetings but the afternoon was free. It was unusually warm for October and Warren invited me to join him in a stroll around the local market. I happily agreed as I wanted to buy some gifts for the children. We stopped from time to time for a chat with fellow AA members who were easily identified by the name badges we all wore. The narrow streets were full of recovering alcoholics from all over the country and there was much good natured banter wherever we went. We have a saying in AA: "There are no strangers in AA, only friends you haven't met before".

After I had bought some gifts for the children we walked down to the river where the trees were ablaze with autumn colours and the vivid shades of red and orange made a beautiful backdrop to the fast flowing river. As we strolled along in the sunshine Warren began to share a little of his story with me.

After a difficult childhood Warren left home and joined the Merchant Navy. He spent many years travelling the world and enjoying life before the scourge of alcoholism finally caught up with him. Like me, he had tried to blot out unhappy memories with alcohol but like all alcoholics he finally realised that alcohol only made things worse; nothing was solved by trying to run away from the past. Finally, at the early age of twenty-one he was hospitalised whilst his ship was docked in Japan with alcohol poisoning. When he was released from the hospital the company he worked for flew him home but he was discharged from service on the grounds of his alcoholism. His life rapidly went downhill from that point until he finally arrived at the doors of AA at the age of twenty-five. At least he had never married, which was just as well because relationships don't have much chance of success when they take second place to alcohol.

After chatting for several hours Warren and I strolled back to the bed and breakfast as it would soon be time to get ready for the evening's entertainment. After the AA meeting, there was to be a ceilidh in the hall which promised to be fun. A ceilidh is a lively Scottish sing-along cum dance, and it was indeed an evening packed with fun and laughter and I couldn't remember when I'd laughed so much. I had felt so depressed and unhappy for so long that it was a real tonic just to be able to let go and enjoy myself. The evening was a lot of fun and the hall was packed with people having a great time, soft drinks in hand. Passers-by could be forgiven for thinking there must have been a wild drunken party going on.

"Aren't you glad you came?" laughed Joan. "Yes, I am." I replied but little did either of us know that my life would never be the same after that fateful weekend.

When the Sunday morning meeting finished, Warren and I went for a final stroll by the river. We didn't have much to say as we watched the fallen leaves float downstream. Another season was coming to end, just like this magical weekend. I felt sad as I said goodbye to Warren. On the journey home my heart was heavy as I realised I would probably never see him again and I was going back to an unhappy marriage. If it wasn't for my children I would have ended it all but I just couldn't do that to them, although what I did next was pretty drastic.

Three weeks after I got back from Dumfries, I was surprised one evening to receive a phone call from Warren. "I can't get you out of my mind," he said. "I just keep thinking about how unhappy you are." I admitted that I had been thinking a lot about him too and the wonderful weekend we had shared. My mind was in turmoil. What could I do? I knew my marriage was over but I didn't have the courage to do anything about it.

"Look Margaret, why don't we meet up somewhere? Let's at least talk things over face to face?" It was difficult with us living so far apart but finally, after weeks of agonising I agreed to Warren's suggestion that we meet up in Blackpool to discuss our situation.

I have never felt so wretched or guilty as I did that November morning. I hurriedly threw a few clothes into a small overnight bag before dropping the children off at their schools. Dashing home, I hastily scribbled a note for David telling him I was going away for a couple of days to sort myself out, and not to worry about me. Then, taking a taxi to the station, I just managed to catch the train before it pulled out. If I had missed that train I would never have had the courage to wait around for the next one. I spent most of the journey staring miserably out of the window. My thoughts were racing. What would the children think? I couldn't believe what I was doing. How could I possibly justify it?

I will never forget the sight of Warren waiting anxiously for me at the barrier of the station in Blackpool. He looked pretty miserable too. Neither of us was very happy about the situation but we knew this was the only way to sort out our feelings for each other. We found rooms in a small bed and breakfast place - not hard to find in Blackpool in winter - and after dropping our bags off we set out along the sea front.

Although it was early November the promenade was busy. A brass band competition was taking place in the town and there was a lively atmosphere despite the cold wind blowing in from the sea. As we strolled along the blustery promenade we tried to sort out our emotions. One thing was obvious; despite having only recently met, we felt as though we'd known each other for years and a deep affection and sense of trust had already sprung up between us. I felt a strange mixture of emotions; happiness that we were together again and misery about the complicated circumstances. Things looked impossible from where I was standing but Warren was the eternal optimist.

"One day I'm going to marry you," he said as we walked along the windswept promenade. "Just you wait. I'm sure things will work out for us."

I thought he was quite mad. How could he possibly even think about marriage, given our circumstances? David would be arriving home to a cryptic note and would no doubt be worried sick about me. In fact his first reaction was to phone the police who tried to reassure him that as I had left a note I could not be considered a 'missing person' and would probably show up again in a day or two.

As we walked along the seafront surrounded by throngs of happy people it just seemed to highlight our turmoil. Taking shelter in a little café we spent hours agonising over the situation trying to find a solution. I knew I could not in all honesty continue in my marriage and whether or not it worked out for Warren and me I would have to make the break with David. Warren was merely the catalyst, not the cause of the breakup.

We finally agreed that I should go home and face David with the truth: there was no alternative. I dislike deceit in any form and decided to go back and sort things out face to face with my husband. He was a decent man and deserved to be told the truth. However, when I spoke to him from a call box in the shadow of Blackpool Tower, it was obvious the time was not right for this. He was furious with me and breathing dire threats. And any courage I had mustered to make the phone call disappeared when I heard my sister's angry voice in the background and I knew that if I went back at that point I would never have the nerve to leave again and would be forced to continue living a lie.

"You can't go back there just now. They're so angry with you. I'm so afraid that if you leave now I'll never see you again!"

Warren persuaded me that the only course of action at present was for me to accompany him to Aberdeen until things had cooled down a little at home. "Give them time to get used to the idea and wait until their anger has died down" Warren said. And so it was with much trepidation and a heavy heart that I set off for Aberdeen.

What I was doing went against all my principles and I was wracked with guilt. On the one hand I was so happy with Warren; I had at last met somebody who understood me and for the first time in my life I felt totally accepted and loved just as I was. But how could I expect the children to understand?

I gazed miserably out at the Cumbrian hills as we sped north, heading further and further away from my children and by the time we reached Aberdeen my resolve was weakening. "I can't leave the kids!" I cried. Jumping out of the car I ran into a phone box and called David. I begged him to let me at least speak to the children. I could hear them crying in the background. He reluctantly agreed and although it was distressing for all of us, I managed to tell them both that I loved them and promised I would try to see them as soon as possible.

I arrived in Aberdeen with nothing but the contents of a

small holdall and the clothes I was wearing. As I gazed out of the window at the grey granite buildings, I thought back to the last time I was in the city. As a thirteen year old schoolgirl I had spent two very happy weeks in Aberdeen with a classmate who invited me to stay with her relatives in the city. As my mother had not been able to afford holidays, travelling to Scotland was an exciting adventure for me. I had loved Aberdeen and vowed that someday I would return. But I could never have imagined under what circumstances that vow would be fulfilled.

For the first couple of weeks we stayed with one of Warren's friends and his wife. I was desperately unhappy and missed the children so much that each time I phoned them, it became harder not to dash straight back home to them.

"Margaret, if you go back now I'll never see you again. I promise you, things will work out fine. Give David some more time before you go and see him." I didn't share Warren's optimism; as far as I could see, the whole situation was a disaster and it would take a miracle to put it right. Being separated from my children became unbearable and I made up my mind that I would just leave and go back to them. But just when I'd decided to leave, circumstances changed and I was faced with another decision.

One evening about three weeks after I arrived in Aberdeen, Warren came in from work with the news that he was being transferred to Rotterdam. "It will only be for a couple of months I promise you" he said, as I began to find reasons why I couldn't possibly go. He gazed out of the window for a moment before he turned and said: "Now we know why you brought your passport." I put the kettle on while he continued: "Why would anyone take a passport for a weekend in Blackpool?" It was true; I'd been surprised to find my passport at the bottom of my overnight bag. I have no idea to this day how it came to be there. It had seemed odd but I thought no more of it until now. It was certainly providential for I could not have gone to Holland without it. "You were meant to bring it, that's for sure" Warren said thoughtfully. I believe that had I not left the UK at that point I would probably have gone back to the marriage for the sake of the children which would have been disastrous for all concerned.

My thoughts were in turmoil as we drove to Hull to catch the overnight ferry to Rotterdam. Although I was happy with Warren, being away from the children was tearing me apart and each phone call left me feeling more wretched.

We found an apartment to rent in Rotterdam and I went to work alongside Warren in his new office. But I soon discovered that nothing had really changed and I had just brought my problems along with me. I knew that I would soon have to go and see David and the children and face up to things honestly. Finally in March, Warren and I took the ferry across to Hull where David and the children were waiting for me. With much trepidation, Warren watched as I got into the car with David, not sure whether he would ever see me again.

It was a very tearful reunion for all of us and a difficult journey home. During the next couple of days, David and I discussed matters in a calm, rational manner and he finally accepted that the marriage was over. He generously agreed that the children could spend the school holidays with me in Aberdeen and he even said that he would let them stay with me if that was what they wanted. I felt deeply sad as we said goodbye for the last time and I truly hoped that he would meet somebody who would love him as he deserved to be loved. What made it worse was that David insisted that he still loved me and that he always would. It made it even more difficult to leave but I knew that staying out of a sense of guilt or pity was not the answer.

After several more weeks in Rotterdam, the office was finally established to the company's satisfaction and Warren handed things over to local staff. We went back to Aberdeen where we managed to find a flat to rent. I couldn't bear to stay home every day, plagued as I was guilt and doubt so I took a secretarial job in the city in an effort to crowd out my confused emotions. The strain of being separated from my children began to affect my health. I was smoking heavily and losing weight rapidly, hitting an all time low of seven stones. My doctor became quite concerned and issued me with a prescription for anti-depressants. I was desperately torn between wanting to stay with Warren and feeling guilty and miserable about leaving the children. I knew I could not go on like this for much longer: I was on the verge of a nervous breakdown. Before long, however, things would get even worse.

CHAPTER TEN

Once More into the Valley

He who conceals his sins does not prosper,
but whoever confesses and renounces them finds mercy
(Proverbs 28: 13)

One evening in late June 1979, David phoned me. After exchanging a few pleasantries, he suddenly became serious. "Margaret, you know I will always love you," he said, "but I guess the marriage really is over isn't it? I want you to know the children can come and live with you if they want to because you were always a good mother and that's where they belong. I hope we'll always be friends Margaret, and one day perhaps I'll even be ready to meet Warren. I don't think I could handle it right now, but one day I hope I can." I was touched by David's generosity of spirit.

"David I'll never be able to thank you enough for that." I said "and I deeply regret the hurt I've caused you." There was an awkward silence, we were both very emotional.

After agreeing on the details for the children's visit to Aberdeen, we said our goodbyes. As I put the phone down I felt deeply grateful for David's kindness and once again was flooded with regret that I had hurt him so much. But I was thankful that at least the children could spend their summer holidays with me and I began to make excited plans.

About a week later I was woken early by the insistent ringing of the phone. My heart sank, early morning phone calls usually mean only one thing – bad news. It was my sister Betty and she got straight to the point. "I'm sorry Margaret. There's no easy way to say this; I'm afraid David is dead."

I felt as though a ton of concrete had been poured into my body and despite the early morning sun, the room suddenly felt chilly. This was a nightmare; how could David be dead? He was only thirty-five years old, surely it couldn't be true? I struggled to take the information in. Apparently David had been in perfectly good health when he went to bed but had suffered an epileptic fit whilst he was asleep and choked to death. His mother Katie, who had been staying there, had been woken when he fell out of bed but by the time she reached him it was too late. My heart went out to her; David was her only child and she idolised him. I knew she would be devastated.

Hurriedly throwing a few clothes into a bag, I left for Barrow immediately. I had to reach the children as soon as possible. I can't remember anything about the drive down, I was so overwrought. I tried to imagine the children and their bewilderment. They had been taken to my sister's house and when I arrived they were standing forlornly at the window, waiting for me; the sight of their sad little faces is still imprinted on my memory.

The unspoken question hung in the air. "Why?" What could I say? I had asked myself that same question ever since I left home that morning. Perhaps they wondered why their Dad had died instead of me, the one who had left them. I certainly did. I was sure this was God's way of punishing me for deserting my family and I believed I deserved it. But the children didn't deserve to suffer so. I just wished with all my heart that it was me who had died and not David. But that was in God's hands, not mine.

There were many arrangements to be made after the post-mortem had taken place. My mother-in-law asked me if I had any objections to David being buried in Aberfan cemetery. I was touched and surprised that she asked me as I really didn't feel entitled to make such a decision. I knew it meant a lot to her and readily agreed.

"You will be there won't you?" she said rather anxiously. "He never stopped loving you, you know?" I felt terrible. What could I say? Of course I wanted to be at David's funeral but at the same time I felt so guilty and ashamed of what I'd done that I dreaded it. I knew I could expect cold and hostile treatment and I was right. The one person who had most right to be angry and bitter was my mother-in-law Katie, but in fact she was kindness itself. David had inherited her generous nature.

It was a sad little procession which made the journey from Barrow to South Wales. Naturally, nobody was too keen to speak to me at the funeral and I was shunned like a pariah. I suppose they blamed me for David's death; I certainly blamed myself. I felt completely isolated, with nobody to share my grief with. I understood why people were angry with me but I too felt a deep sense of loss.

David was a good and kind man and the father of my children and I had so hoped that he would go on to find happiness with somebody else but it was not to be. I remembered our recent conversation when he had so generously offered to send the children up to Aberdeen and I marvelled at the timing. At least I knew that he had forgiven me and harboured no bitterness and I will be eternally grateful for his generosity of spirit. I wept, too, for my children's loss, knowing only too well the pain of losing your Dad as a child.

The weeks that followed are hazy. Simon who was now eleven and Sara nine, came to live with us in Aberdeen and both settled in remarkably well, considering the big changes they had to cope with. Warren handled the situation extremely well, realising how hurt they were and how they might resent him.

"We don't have to change our name do we Mum?" asked Simon anxiously. "No of course you don't" Warren reassured him. He realised how important it was that the children keep their father's name. "David was your Dad Simon and nobody can take his place." Despite his lack of experience with children, Warren's genuine kindness soon won the children over and they realised he was not trying to replace their father. Children are very resilient, and provided they are loved and in a stable environment adapt quickly to new situations.

Warren began to talk about getting married but I was reluctant. Not because I didn't love him but because I was still wracked with guilt and felt that I didn't deserve happiness. I was sure that God was angry with me and I was afraid of what might happen if I married again.

Eventually Warren persuaded me but this time I insisted on a Registry Office wedding. Whilst I knew that as a widow I was entitled to get married in the Catholic Church, I was so ashamed of what I had done that I felt to marry in church would be hypocritical. The truth was I hated myself and didn't feel worthy to receive the sacrament of marriage when I had failed so miserably to keep my vows. But God had other plans.

Although I had stopped attending Mass because of my guilty conscience, I dropped the children off each Sunday outside the local church and picked them up after Mass. One day the Parish Priest pounced on me as I was collecting the children, saying that he would like to have a 'little chat' with me. Assuming that he meant some vague time in the distant future, I agreed and was totally unprepared when he suggested that I come to the presbytery at five-thirty that evening! I didn't have time to think of an excuse. Besides, he was a somewhat forceful old Jesuit so I rather lamely agreed.

For the rest of that day I was a nervous wreck. What on earth did he want? And what was I going to say to him? If I told him my story he would probably be horrified and give me a lecture; I didn't need anybody else to tell me how sinful I was: I told myself that every day and I didn't relish having a priest threatening me with hellfire and damnation, especially a Jesuit!

As I rang the doorbell at the presbytery that evening I felt physically sick and utterly miserable. After settling down into a worn old armchair with a cup of strong tea and a cigarette, I poured out my story. Something about the old priest told me it would not be a good idea to lie to him and so I told him the whole sorry tale, leaving nothing out. When I had finally run out of steam, Father Myles looked at me with such compassion that I felt quite overwhelmed. Instead of judging and condemning me he invited me to make my confession, reminding me that Jesus himself had said that he came for sinners not the righteous.

"I rather suspect He meant the self-righteous" he chuckled, "because nobody is actually righteous in the sight of God. Even the best of us are pretty awful!" He smiled kindly.

"But Father, I left my children! I deserted my marriage! How can God forgive that? I don't deserve to be forgiven!" "No dear, you are quite right!" he smiled. "None of us 'deserves' to be forgiven actually. But God is merciful and He loves us, despite our weaknesses. That's why He sent Jesus to die in our place. My dear, I've noticed you each week when you collect the children and you look as though you have the weight of the world on your shoulders! Yes, you did wrong my dear, but now it's time to put the past behind you and make a fresh start! You simply can't spend the rest of your life punishing yourself. That's not the Lord telling you how awful you are. That's the devil!"

I was startled at his mention of the devil. As far as I was concerned, it was all my fault and I had no desire to blame anybody else, even the devil! I had never heard a priest speak like that before and whilst I didn't understand his theology, I was deeply touched by his kindness.

After hearing my confession, Father Myles blessed me and told me to be sure and come to mass the following Sunday. Once my marriage had been formally blessed by the Church I would be able to receive the Eucharist too. I walked out of there feeling as though a great burden had been lifted from my shoulders, as indeed it had. My sins had weighed me down and it was good to be told that God had forgiven me. Whilst I was not totally convinced, it was a start.

Within a short time I received a letter from the Bishop of Aberdeen informing me that arrangements had been made to have my marriage regularised in accordance with Canon Law. I was delighted and Warren who had watched my health deteriorate, readily agreed to have our marriage blessed in church. I think he would have agreed to anything that would relieve the awful guilt which was destroying me.

When we spoke to Fr. Myles, it transpired that the next available date he had free was the eighteenth of October, which by one of those strange 'coincidences' just happened to be our first wedding anniversary. And so exactly one

year after our Registry Office wedding, Warren and I
finally received the Church's blessing. Although I was
happy to receive this official blessing, deep down I still felt
that I didn't deserve happiness and even if God had
forgiven me, I couldn't forgive myself.

For the next few years I must have been an absolute
nightmare to live with and most men would have given up
on me. I believe Warren must have received a special grace
to put up with my wild mood swings and depression.

Through sheer will power I kept a tight lid on my emotions
and hid my true feelings from the rest of the world. I went
to work each day and acted as if everything was fine. Once
more I was wearing a mask and it was an Oscar winning
performance. After a days work I would travel home on
the bus but the moment I reached home the mask came off
and I broke down and wept. Most evenings Warren came
home to find me in floods of tears. How he tolerated it I will
never know. He deserved a medal for staying with me and
trying to keep the family together and I thank God for his
loyalty. Simon and Sara could only look on helplessly and I
couldn't possibly explain to them what was happening. I
didn't understand it myself. My nerves were at breaking
point and I didn't know where to turn for help.

In desperation, Warren phoned Father Myles, who
suggested a short retreat might help. Reluctantly I agreed
to give it a try and several weeks later I found myself at
St. Mary's Redemptorist centre at Kinnoull, Perth. I
didn't know what I was letting myself in for, but I was so
desperate I was willing to try anything, even if that meant

spending a boring weekend with strangers in a gloomy
monastery. In fact St. Mary's was anything but gloomy; it
was a warm and welcoming place and the silent retreat I
had envisioned turned out to be a very lively weekend, full
of fun and laughter. Little did I know it, but I'd just had an
'accidental encounter' with Catholic Charismatic Renewal.
God had sneaked up on me!

The theme of the retreat was based on a verse from the book
of Isaiah: 'Does a woman forget her baby or fail to love
the child of her womb? Even if these forget, I will never
forget you, for I have carved your name on the palm of my
hand. (Isaiah 49: 15-16)

Like many Catholics, I was not familiar with the bible and I
couldn't remember hearing those words before. However,
they touched me deeply as I remembered only too well the
very words I'd spoken to my own baby on the day I had
handed her over to strangers when I'd assured her that I
would never forget her. Yes, I knew only too well that a
mother never forgets her baby. Not a day had gone by since
I'd parted with my baby when I didn't think about her and
wonder where she was. I longed to know if she was safe and
well and whether her adoptive parents loved her as I did.
However according to the law, I had no legal rights to any
information about my child and I could not even discover
whether she was alive or dead. But to my way of thinking,
this was just part of the punishment I had brought on
myself for my sin and I certainly didn't think I deserved any
sympathy. I had heaped sin upon sin and now I was paying
the price.

The turning point came that weekend when I had a frank discussion with the priest who was leading the retreat and told him as honestly as I could about my past. He asked me if I was sorry for all the wrong things I had done and whether I believed God had forgiven me.

"Of course I'm sorry Father" I said rather crossly, "but what good is that? Nothing can change the past, can it? I can't undo all the harm I've done, can I? So sorry's not enough!" He looked at me kindly. "No, Margaret, you can't undo the past; but God can heal it. He's the same yesterday, today and forever. All time belongs to him, and whether it is the past, the present or the future makes no difference to God." I remained unconvinced.

He continued: "Yes, you did sin, but you must believe that when we repent, God immediately forgives us. Our problem is that often other people may throw our wrong-doing back in our face and refuse to forgive us, and we project their unforgiveness onto God. Another problem is that sometimes we can't seem to forgive ourselves and I think that's why you're so unhappy. You must accept God's forgiveness Margaret, and stop punishing yourself. Jesus died for your sins and there's no way you can pay that debt. Forgiveness is a free gift and God wants to pour his healing grace upon you but you have to accept it Margaret. It was through the grace of God that your marriage to Warren was blessed by the church; you didn't even know that was possible did you? Can't you see how God's been helping you? He's been using your parish priest to bless you but you must be willing to receive His love. He wants to set you free from the things of the past which are holding you back and destroying your peace. It's not God who's punishing you Margaret, it's you! Now it's time to move on and ask God to help you let go of the past and be the best wife and mother you can be from now on. You know, the devil loves to remind us of our sins. He likes nothing better than to tell us how rotten we are!" Well I'd had enough and I couldn't take any more. I desperately needed the peace that only God can give and I was willing to try anything.

I had never experienced anybody laying hands on me before and I was startled when Father Bev laid his hand upon my head and said a short prayer for me and my family. He asked the Lord to set me free and although I didn't understand what he meant by 'set free,' I felt a glimmer of hope for the future. For the first time in my life I felt a tangible sense of peace and I went home feeling much better.

Corrie Ten Boom in her wonderful book 'The Hiding Place' says: "When we tell God we are sorry for our sins, He takes them and dumps them in a deep lake and puts up a sign saying: 'No Fishing'". I realised I had been poking around in my 'lake' of guilt for years and it was not God who constantly reminded me of my sins but myself and, if Fr. Bev was to believed, perhaps the devil had a hand in it too?

A few days after the retreat weekend, I was invited back to Kinnoull to attend a healing service led by an American priest, Father Robert DeGrandis.

"Oh, I don't need healing thanks. My health is fine.

Lourdes and all that stuff is not my thing." I'm afraid the cynic in me dismissed the suggestion immediately as I pictured a church filled with people in wheelchairs or on crutches being manipulated by some hyped-up American priest.

"Well actually Margaret, it's not just physical healing we're talking about. We all need inner healing and that's what last weekend was really all about." Helen Smith, the lady who had organised the retreat, was persistent and I decided to humour her. "Oh all right then. I'll come!"

It was the first healing service I'd ever attended and it was unforgettable. The church was packed and there was a buzz in the air. It was obvious we were in for something very different from our usual Sunday Mass. The priest breezed in with typical American brashness and I thought, "Oh no! Get me out of here! He'll have us shouting 'Hallelujah! Praise the Lord' next!" If I'd come down to Perth in my own car I would have left immediately but as I had travelled down with a group from Aberdeen I was stuck. We were ninety miles from home and I'd just have to grit my teeth and sit it out.

Father DeGrandis had a vibrant personality and a lively manner and was quite unlike any priest I had met before. He was bouncing with joy and his joy was infectious and soon I put my prejudices to one side. After Mass he invited everybody to come forward for prayer and although I had no desire to be prayed with, I found myself being pushed forward in the eager crowd. I felt a bit of a fraud as I stood in line next to people who had obvious physical disabilities; after all I wasn't sick, was I? I didn't realise at that point just how sick I was, emotionally and spiritually. I was not prepared for what happened next.

As I stood in line Father DeGrandis laid his hand gently on my forehead and I was immediately aware of a brilliant white light accompanied by a powerful but gentle force which pushed me to the ground. I lay there for some time, fully conscious but feeling as though I was in a place of great peace and restfulness. Although I was aware of what was going on around me, I felt unable to move and just lay there, bathed in an indescribable joy and warmth. When I was finally helped to my feet I returned to my seat in a daze. I hardly spoke a word on the journey home which for me was most unusual! I didn't realise it at the time but I'd been 'resting in the Spirit' and this signaled the beginning of a long, slow process of inner healing.

A few months later I discovered to my delight that I was pregnant. My two older children, by now teenagers, were not exactly thrilled when I told them; I think they were embarrassed, although they were delighted when Michael was born.

The months immediately following were difficult and I felt confused and disappointed. Here I was with a lovely new baby and yet I couldn't really enjoy him. Michael was one of those babies who cry for hours each night and I was suffering from a severe shortage of sleep. Each day I was totally exhausted but I couldn't get any rest. Michael was a very demanding baby and as soon as I laid him down he would cry. I tried to snatch a little sleep whenever I could but it took its toll on me.

When Warren got home from work at night, the house was chaotic. I couldn't keep on top of the housework and the old feelings of failure once more overwhelmed me. Finally my doctor diagnosed post natal depression and suggested a course of anti- depressants. However, before Michael was even three months old I discovered I was pregnant again and I was afraid drugs would harm the unborn baby so I stopped taking the anti-depressants immediately.

My doctor's reaction was very negative: "Of course you can't go through with this pregnancy; you will have to have a termination. If you can't cope with one new baby, how will you cope with two?" he said. I was horrified and I felt very let down. I needed support and the only solution suggested by my doctor was abortion. I told the doctor in no uncertain terms what I thought of that idea. He frowned and shook his head: "Well, I just hope you know what you are doing" he said as I got up to leave. "I'll make an appointment for you to go to the hospital."

I found the same negative attitude when I visited the ante-natal clinic. I felt as though I was doing something terribly wrong, having another baby so soon after Michael's birth, especially as I was almost thirty-eight. The staff were surprised when I told them I did not want any pre-natal testing which might reveal abnormalities in the baby. What was the point? I would not have an abortion no matter what they found. Shrugging dismissively the nurse made it quite plain that she thought that I was being irresponsible. I left the hospital feeling sad. What should have been a joyful occasion was marred by the attitude of the medical staff and I reflected upon how radically things had changed in the years since my first children were born. Now it seemed that it was expected of you to have pre-natal screening to identify 'defects' followed by abortion as a solution to this.

I felt fiercely protective of this new life within me and the pregnancy was in fact an important turning point for me emotionally. I began to look forward eagerly to the birth and coped better with Michael. Warren was naturally concerned about me and how I would manage two babies. "Don't worry," I told him, "God will take care of me." I don't know where those words came from and I was as surprised as Warren was when I heard myself. But I really believed it and tried not to worry about the future.

Shortly before the baby was due, we attended my sister-in-law's wedding in a nearby town. As I stood in the church I began to feel distinctly peculiar and had a horrid suspicion that I was about to go into labour. My waters broke as soon as we left the church and with no time to spare we headed back to Aberdeen. We got some peculiar looks as we parked the car and hurried into the maternity unit. There we were; both dressed in our wedding finery complete with flowers. It was only later that I was told the bemused nursing staff had said to themselves: "Hm, they're cutting it fine aren't they; heading straight from the Church to the labour ward?" We laughed about this afterwards but at the time I just wanted to get in to the hospital and have the baby as fast as possible and I didn't give a thought to how we must have looked.

I was delighted that it was another little boy. As they were so close in ages I thought it was lovely for Michael to have a little brother. Tony was born just two weeks before Michael's first birthday. I can't pretend life was easy with a new baby, a toddler, and two teenagers to cope with but Warren helped as much as possible and the older children soon became dab hands at changing a nappy, experience which I assured them would one day stand them in good stead! In fact as the two younger children were growing into lively toddlers I couldn't have coped without the help of Simon and Sara. Sara in particular bore the brunt of the child minding and I will always be grateful for her help.

Life had certainly improved dramatically since the night of the healing service. Although I didn't understand what had actually happened that night, I was relieved to be free of the insidious guilt which had plagued me for so long. I attended Mass faithfully each Sunday, although I can't say it had much real impact on my life; it was just a habit really and I was conscious that I went mostly from a sense of 'obligation.' It was something that Catholics did on a Sunday.

Despite the fact that I had a good husband and four lovely children the nagging thought persisted; 'there must be more to life than this!' I was conscious of an inner void. What on earth was wrong with me? Would I ever have peace of mind? Or was I destined to spend the rest of my life an emotional misfit?

CHAPTER ELEVEN

Free at Last

I will give you a new heart
and put a new spirit in you
(Ezekiel 36: 26)

One Sunday morning during Mass, when I was feeling particularly hopeless words from the first reading suddenly broke into my wandering thoughts: "I shall give you a new heart, and put a new spirit in you; I shall remove the heart of stone from your bodies and give you a heart of flesh instead." (Ezekiel 36: 26)

I was astonished because recently I had been reflecting on my feelings of emptiness. It seemed to me that I had an emotional blockage of some kind. It was as though something prevented me from really connecting with those I loved and I remembered thinking: "I must have a stone where my heart should be?" This particular Sunday, for once the readings actually penetrated the fog in my mind

137

and I was stunned: it was uncannily accurate as though God was speaking directly to me.

During the following week I kept remembering the words I'd heard at Mass. Was it just a coincidence or could God possibly have known how hopeless I felt, and was trying to get my attention? I knew that they were just the regular Sunday readings scheduled for that day but I was struck by the timing. They coincided perfectly with how I felt about myself; they had penetrated my mind and deeply affected me. Apart from hearing the scriptures read at mass, I had no experience of reading the bible. In fact whenever I had tried briefly to read it, I had quickly put it down again as it made little sense to me. The Old Testament particularly seemed to be full of people with unpronounceable names doing incomprehensible things! And as far as I was concerned, it was totally irrelevant to my everyday life. I found it utterly confusing and after starting in Genesis, I gave up shortly after Noah came out of the Ark!

I am embarrassed now when I think of how ignorant I was but I suppose many people go to church each week but don't actually expect God to touch their lives in any way, and I was no exception. But during that week as I reflected on the 'heart of stone', which I certainly identified with, I said a rather desperate prayer: "God, if you are there and if you do care, please help me. I can't go on like this."

But God, if He had heard me did not respond. Why should He? Several months passed and I continued to go through the motions, trying to be a good wife and mother and just getting on with life. The difference was, instead of saying the usual set, formal prayers; I simply used my own rather desperate words.

"God if you are real then where are you? Please do something! If I don't hear from you pretty soon I'm just going to pack all this religion in. It's pointless!" As far as I was concerned it was all or nothing. My patience was running out and I made up my mind that unless I had a breakthrough of some kind, I would abandon all thoughts of God and religion.

During this period, mortgage rates were at their highest level in years and I had been reluctantly forced to return to full-time work, leaving the boys in the care of a childminder. What with working full time and taking care of the family, I didn't have much time to dwell on spiritual matters; I was too busy trying to make ends meet. However, the nagging feeling that there must be more to life than this persisted, and I grew increasingly desperate.

Shortly before Valentine's Day 1985, I went out during my lunch hour to buy a Valentine's card for Warren. I must confess my motives were pretty base. As Warren was in London on business, I was sure he would not have bought me a card, and I wanted to make him feel guilty! I don't know why I didn't go into W.H. Smith's, the nearest shop but for some reason I walked straight past and headed up to the Church of Scotland Bookshop. I had never been in a Christian bookshop in my life and as I walked through the doors I felt self-conscious and awkward, as if I had 'Roman Catholic' printed on my forehead! I had met hostility in the past from other Christians who, once they discovered I was a Catholic, implied that I was not a 'real Christian' and therefore not 'saved.' Unless I left the Catholic Church I was a lost cause as far as they were concerned!

However, overcoming my embarrassment I went in and browsed the shelves. After choosing an appropriate card I stood in line waiting to pay for it and as I glanced at the rows of books, one particular title caught my eye. It was called: 'I Dared to Call Him Father: The Miraculous Story of a Muslim Woman's Encounter with God' by Bilquis Sheikh. I was intrigued. I didn't know much about Islam but I was curious. If a Muslim woman could have an encounter with God, why not a Catholic woman too? As I turned the slim paperback over back in my hand I realised that I'd never actually read a Christian book before! In fact I didn't know such things existed.

Back at the office, my boss who was a committed Baptist noticed the book with its distinctive cover sitting on my desk. "Oh. That looks interesting Margaret." He said. The cover depicted a Muslim woman peeping shyly from beneath her veil. "Tell you what. When you've read it, why not bring it in and I'll give it to my wife Sheila, she has lots of Christian books and I'm sure she'd be glad to do a swap." I found the book so fascinating that it didn't take me long to finish it and I did a swap with my boss who gave me a book entitled: 'Fear No Evil' by David Watson, and another piece of the jigsaw fell into place.

The name David Watson meant nothing to me at that point, but I discovered he was a well known Anglican minister whose church, St. Michael le Belfry in York had been on the brink of being turned into a museum but instead, had experienced an extraordinary spiritual revival. The book was a moving account of David's battle with cancer and by the time I read the last page I was in tears as I read that he had died a little over a year previously. As I read about his struggle with the disease, I'd been desperately hoping there would be a happy ending and that God would miraculously heal him; but it was not to be.

The night I finished reading the book, I was in the house alone, apart from the little ones who were fast asleep. Warren had gone to an AA meeting and the older children were out with their friends. As I closed the book I suddenly felt an overwhelming urge to kneel down and thank God for letting David Watson live long enough to write that book. It is difficult to describe spiritual experiences but what happened next is still as vivid more than twenty years later as it was that February night in 1985.

I knelt down and closing my eyes I suddenly found myself in a place of indescribable brightness. It was as though I were a spectator in a huge open space where there were literally thousands of people dressed in white. They were worshipping God; although obviously I couldn't see Him I sensed His presence. As I stood there transfixed, I became aware of somebody standing close by. Although I didn't see His face, I knew without doubt that it was Jesus and His presence was so real that I began to weep when He spoke to me. In a gentle yet powerful voice He said: "This is your Father, and He loves you." His presence overwhelmed me and I was filled with an intense joy. Not only did Jesus know me completely, but He loved me despite my faults and failings.   For the first time in my life I felt truly loved and accepted and I felt an incredible sense of freedom. Although I knew my husband loved me, I still never actually 'felt' loved deep down inside but now I knew beyond all doubt that God is real and that He truly is my Father who loves me beyond measure. I lost all sense of time and I have no idea how long the experience lasted. When I became aware of my surroundings again, although my face was soaked with tears, I felt an indescribable peace and a sense of freedom as though I'd been released from a dark cell and brought into the light.

This life-changing experience is sometimes referred to as: 'Baptism in the Holy Spirit.' It is difficult to find words to adequately describe it but the result was immediate and permanent. From that moment I never doubted the reality of the existence of God and that He is indeed our Father. Jesus said: 'No one knows the Father except the Son and those to whom the Son chooses to reveal him' (Mat 11:27). Why it happened when it did I may never know, but that night, Jesus chose to reveal the Father to me and transformed my life forever.

I was so overwhelmed with joy that I felt like running up and down the street knocking on doors and asking everybody: "Hey, did you know Jesus is alive and He really loves us?" However reason told me that most people would just think I was certifiably insane!

When Warren got home that night he looked at me with a puzzled expression. "What have you been doing to yourself? You look different; your face seems to be glowing." But the experience was so profound and intimate that I didn't feel able to describe to Warren what had happened that night and mumbled some excuse. He told me later that he was a little afraid I'd really gone 'over the top' this time. It was some time before I felt able to share my experience with Warren and although he said he believed me, I'm sure he thought I was imagining things. Religious experiences are very difficult to share because they are so subjective and I don't blame anybody for being sceptical. All I know is that my life changed forever on the seventeenth of February, 1985.

Mornings were never my best time of day and I usually felt sluggish first thing in the morning but during the following week I woke up at six o'clock each morning feeling refreshed and raring to go. After a few days of waking up like this I wondered if God was waking me up. I know this sounds fanciful but I couldn't think of any other explanation; it was so far removed from my usual pattern. I decided to put it to the test, after all I had nothing to lose. So I asked God to confirm whether it really was Him waking me up or just my imagination.

The next morning I got up at six o'clock and went downstairs to see if God would give me some kind of sign. Feeling slightly ridiculous, I put the kettle on and waited for God to show up. I didn't know what to expect, but I was not going to go without my morning cup of tea and I hoped God wouldn't mind if I had a cigarette as well! I can't imagine what God must have thought, looking down on me with a cup of tea in one hand and a cigarette in the other! But I have a feeling He smiled; at least I was taking Him seriously.

'What happens now?' I thought as I sat there drinking my tea. I am not sure quite what I expected but I sat there with the minutes ticking by feeling more and more foolish. It must have been my imagination after all. What did I expect; an angel with a message from God? Feeling rather disappointed I decided to go back to my nice warm bed and put such foolish notions behind me. Suddenly the thought occurred to me, perhaps I might find some answers in the bible; after all, it was a reading from scripture which had triggered this whole thing. I crept upstairs to fetch my bible, certain that if he saw me Warren would think I had really flipped, creeping round in the dark clutching a bible! Not knowing where to start looking I opened it at random and immediately read these words: "At daybreak you hear my voice; at daybreak I lay my case before you." (Psalm 5: 1-3)

That seemed hopeful! The next scripture I came upon was Isaiah 54: 4, which was especially poignant for me:

"Do not be afraid, you will not be put to shame, do not be dismayed, you will not be disgraced: for you will forget the shame of your youth and no longer remember the curse of your widowhood. For now your creator will be your husband ......"

I wept as I felt the impact of those words in my heart. It spoke so clearly and unmistakably into my situation and I was deeply touched. Was it possible that God could speak to us today through scriptures that were written so long ago? I was determined to read the bible as much as I could, even taking it in to the office. During my lunch break I found a quiet corner where I could read without interruption. I soon became a valued customer at the Christian bookshop and read every book I could lay hands on about the Holy Spirit and spiritual growth. It was like suddenly being plunged from a black and white world into a technicolour one, like the scene in the Wizard of Oz where Dorothy is whisked from the monochrome dullness of Kansas to the colourful world of Oz!

My appetite for the things of God was insatiable. I began to attend weekday mass whenever possible and receiving the Eucharist took on a whole new meaning. I wanted to learn as much as possible and I was dying to share it with others. The sad thing was that I felt unable to tell my fellow Catholics about what had happened to me. When I tentatively tried to share my experience, I encountered scepticism and cynicism and several people actually laughed in my face. I soon learned to keep my mouth shut in the company of my fellow parishioners.

In my hunger to share with other Christians I began to visit Pentecostal churches where there was lively, vibrant worship and powerful preaching of the Word. Also they had a strong sense of community and were not afraid or embarrassed to talk about God whereas Catholics would squirm with embarrassment if I tried to share anything spiritual. It was alright to talk about parish bingo or horse-racing nights and socials but anything vaguely spiritual caused them to turn and head for the door! I was desperate to meet others who wanted to grow spiritually and I was tempted to join another church; had I not encountered the F.I.R.E. Rally I might have done so.

The acronym F.I.R.E. represented Faith; Intercession; Repentance and Evangelism and the F.I.R.E. Alliance as the organisation was known, was an American based resource set up in order to help Catholics deepen their faith and grow into a new awareness of the work of the Holy Spirit. In 1985, I attended a F.I.R.E. conference in Edinburgh, a conference which had a powerful impact upon me. The speakers were really inspiring and I had never heard people talk about God with such passion and conviction. I'm embarrassed to admit that I was so ignorant that I actually lit up a cigarette during the conference! I did wonder why one of the speakers gave me a rather strange look but nobody told me that it was not appropriate to smoke and I didn't know any better: the Lord really had His work cut out with me!

At this conference there were hundreds of Catholics unashamedly praising and worshipping the Lord with great joy and freedom. The concluding Mass was celebrated in a way that I'd never experienced before. During the conference I witnessed a great and tangible outpouring of the Holy Spirit, when people of all ages including many priests and religious sisters were so filled with joy that they danced in the aisles, many of them were elderly, so it could hardly be attributed to youthful exuberance! It was an astonishing and unforgettable sight.

Soon after this I joined a small Charismatic Prayer Group which met weekly in the city and it was during my time in that group that my faith began to deepen and I learned about the gifts of the Holy Spirit. Although the group was small in numbers, they were very enthusiastic and deeply committed and what was more, they too had experienced the Baptism of the Holy Spirit.

Although I'd had a bible for about ten years I hardly ever opened it and when I did, I couldn't make much sense of it. My bible is itself a powerful testament to God's love and provision because even whilst I was still in the depths of alcoholism, He provided me with a bible in a most wonderful way through the love of a child.

Whilst we were living in Merthyr Tydfil I used to go along to Sunday Mass feeling hung over from the effects of too much alcohol the night before. After Mass I would often visit the bookstall and perhaps buy a prayer card or holy picture. There was a Jerusalem Bible there which attracted me and I would pick it up each week and leaf carefully through it. I was tempted to buy it but as it cost two pounds I decided it was too expensive, preferring to spend the money on four bottles of cider, which I could buy for the same price. Sadly my need for booze was greater than my need for the Word of God in those days but God loved me despite this.

On Christmas Day in 1975, Simon who was about seven years old then, handed me a carrier bag with The Jerusalem bible in it. He had watched my weekly ritual when I would pick it up, flick through it, and then replace it on the rack. He decided to buy it for me for Christmas, spending all of his money in the process. He didn't realise of course what the book was; he only knew it as that 'big blue book.' When he handed it to me on Christmas morning, he had even bundled it up somewhat clumsily in wrapping paper. I wept when I tore open the wrapping and realised what he'd done.

"Don't you like it Mum?" Simon asked anxiously. What could I say? "Yes, son, it's beautiful. Thank you so much! But what made you spend all your money on it?" He looked at me solemnly with his big brown eyes and said: "Well, Mum I knew you liked it, but you couldn't afford it, because you kept putting it back."

I was deeply touched by Simon's generosity and somewhat ashamed as I knew only too well why I never bought it. I felt duty bound to try to read it after Simon had made such a sacrifice but I couldn't make much sense of it and quickly gave up. The book lay virtually untouched for the next ten years and was in pristine condition.

Today that bible is held together with duct tape and is almost falling apart; it is one of my most treasured possessions and taught me a valuable lesson about God's timing. Despite the fact that I'd preferred to spend my money on alcohol rather than on a bible, God knew that one day I'd be ready to read it and only after I had received His healing touch would I really cherish it.

As I read more and more books written by Christians from different traditions, I realised that deep rifts and misunderstandings had sprang up between Christians since the Reformation. We have constructed denominational walls with our doctrines and dogmas, regarding each other with suspicion and hostility instead of displaying the unity that Jesus so desires. But I cannot forget that God used a former Muslim, a Baptist and an Anglican to touch my heart. I pray that Christian unity will increase and whilst we cannot deny our differences or pretend they don't exist, I long for the day when we truly focus upon what we hold in common, a love for Jesus and a desire to share the Good News with a hurting and broken world.

After my conversion experience, I was desperate for Warren to experience God's love. Although he had been baptised as an infant, Warren was pretty indifferent to religion. He said he believed in God but as he had no formal religious teaching his ideas were pretty vague and woolly. I didn't want my recent experiences to create a barrier between us but like many people who have had a religious experience, I probably went a bit over the top in those early months. I was so excited – I had made the most important discovery of my whole life: God really does exist and He actually loves us! However I had enough sense to know that if I was not careful I would alienate Warren or simply become a terrible bore! He later admitted that he was pretty sure it was just another of my phases which I'd eventually 'get over.' He also said that if he hadn't known better, he would have suspected that I was having an affair! Apparently I looked so much happier and according to him at least, was almost glowing with joy! He also noticed that I'd stopped nagging and in his words: 'became a much nicer person' adding mischievously, "now that really was a miracle!"

"Whatever it was, it must have been pretty powerful to change you like that!" he said. Little did he know that although I was not having an affair, I had in fact fallen head over heels in love with another man, and I would never 'get over it.' But then Jesus was no ordinary man!

"Please God, let Warren experience your love and please help me not to be an obstacle." This was my prayer when I finally realised I was getting nowhere in my efforts to get through to Warren. It was so frustrating not being able to share what had become the most important thing in my life but I knew that my clumsy attempts would have the opposite effect if I wasn't careful

Finally, in sheer frustration I said: "He's your problem Lord. If you want him to know you, then you'll just have to introduce yourself!" I decided to stop preaching to Warren and surrendered him to God; after all it's the Holy Spirit's role to reveal God and convert people, not ours.

In the meantime I read a book called 'The Happiest People on Earth' by Demos Shakarian which tells the fascinating story of how the Full Gospel Businessmen's Fellowship International (F.G.B.M.F.I.) came into being. It began in a small way when a group of Christian businessmen in California decided to meet regularly for breakfast and prayer. That small group of committed prayerful men developed into a flourishing international fellowship, with branches throughout the world. Local groups known as 'Chapters' meet regularly for prayer and every month they hold a dinner in a local hotel and invite guest speakers to share their testimonies.

The aim of the fellowship is to attract those who might not feel comfortable in a church, whereas a local hotel probably seems less threatening and more 'friendly'. Sadly churches and church people have had a bad press and many people would never dream of setting foot in a church because they believe they will be judged and condemned by the self righteous.

I was impressed by what I read about this organisation and was excited to learn there was a chapter in Aberdeen and in fact they would be hosting a dinner the following Saturday. Some friends agreed to come with me but when I invited Warren to join us his answer was an emphatic "No way! That's your scene, not mine." I hid my disappointment as best I could and hoped that he'd have a change of heart.

When Saturday came round it seemed that everything that could possibly go wrong in the house did. The children were fractious all day and Warren, who was not a quarrel-some person, was unusually irritable. I burnt the lunch and to cap it all the cat was sick! I had a terrible headache by teatime and just felt like going off to bed. By the time my friends called for me I was feeling frazzled and in no mood for 'holy stuff.' But when Warren suddenly announced that he was coming after all, I quickly got ready and for once kept my mouth shut!

After a very enjoyable meal in a local hotel our little party proceeded to light up our cigarettes. I did think it odd that there were no ashtrays on the tables but it was a little while before I realised we were the only ones smoking in the whole room and we were attracting some funny looks! Although I've since given up smoking, as a new Christian there were more important issues to be dealt with and it wasn't helpful to feel judged and condemned by other

Christians because I didn't fit their image of how a 'proper' Christian should behave. As a very new Christian I still had a lot of doubts and insecurity and it was hurtful to be treated like a second-rate Christian just because I smoked.

That evening at the F.G.B.M.F.I. dinner, the principal speaker was a rather flamboyant American who told a harrowing tale of drug abuse and imprisonment before he had a vision of Christ and 'got saved' in his prison cell. The testimony was very powerful and moving and I was too enthralled to notice Warren's reaction. The next speaker was a very ordinary man who told a much more mundane story but apparently it was this man's testimony which really touched Warren.

After the talks finished the chairman spoke about committing one's life to Jesus and invited those who wished to do so, to go forward for prayer. He asked us to think about what might happen to us when we died; had we seriously considered where we would spend eternity? He said nobody was actually worthy to spend it with God; this was only possible if we acknowledged we were sinners, repented and invited Jesus Christ to be the Lord of our lives. I watched nervously as Warren shuffled in his seat, expecting him to say it was time to leave.

I had already asked Jesus some months previously to be the Lord of my life. I had made such a mess of it when I was in charge; I really had nothing to lose! I had assumed I was leading a Christian life because I had been baptised and raised as a Catholic and went to Mass each week. However, I began to realise there was more to it than that and I had to

consciously co-operate with God's grace rather than just go
through the religious motions.

After reading David Watson's book, "Fear No Evil," I
decided I wanted to make my own commitment. Whereas
I'd been baptised as an infant, I felt that this was my
parent's decision and now it was time for me as an adult to
make a conscious decision to commit my life to Jesus.
Although I had been confirmed at age twelve, I had no real
understanding of what that meant and besides I still
thought that God only liked 'good' people and was not
interested in the likes of me. And so at the age of thirty-
eight, I knelt down and surrendered my life totally to Jesus
and asked Him to come into my life in a new way. There
were no flashing lights or claps of thunder, but I felt a deep
sense of peace and I felt my life had taken a new direction.
It has been said that Catholics tend to be sacramentalised
but not evangelised and I certainly fell into that category.

When the Chairman of the meeting invited people to come
forward for prayer, a few brave souls responded but I was
sure it was too much to hope that Warren would join them,
and I was astonished when he suddenly got up from his
seat and without a word walked quickly to the front of the
room. I watched in amazement as hands were laid on him
and he began to sway backwards and forwards. I thought
he was going to collapse. He told me later that as the
men laid hands upon him and prayed quietly, he'd felt a
powerful charge of energy surge through his whole body.
As Warren was a very down to earth person, not given to
dramatisation or imagining things, I knew that something
amazing must have happened to him.

That night my prayers were answered, as six months after my conversion experience, Warren too committed his life to Jesus. We talked long into the night and I was overwhelmed with a sense of joy. Warren told me that over the months, as he waited for me to 'come back to normal,' he'd noticed a big change taking place. For instance, whereas I used to be a compulsive worrier I was more relaxed and able to take things in my stride. He said I was much more easy-going and happy. He was both curious and a little afraid: his first thought was that I must be turning into a religious maniac as I always seemed to be reading the bible, and it's a well known fact there are a lot of people in mental hospitals with all kind of religious delusions!

Another thing he noticed was that whereas previously I spent a lot of time each night watching television, I now spent my time reading spiritual books. Previously I would even put the phone off the hook when my favourite soap operas were on, in case somebody disturbed me!

"I couldn't figure it out: you were the same person, yet different," he said. Warren told me later that during the week before the Full Gospel dinner a tremendous battle had been raging in his mind.

"It's a load of rubbish, she's finally cracked!" whispered one voice. "There must be something in it. She's really changed," said another, and he was curious as to what or who had been powerful enough to bring about such changes. Curiosity finally got the better of him and when my friends arrived that evening he just had to see for himself what it was all about.

I believe that when a person is on the verge of conversion to Christ, the enemy, Satan, gets to work too because he hates people to discover the truth and he sows doubts into peoples minds. The devil particularly hates us to be aware of the reality of his existence and that is probably his most powerful weapon – the rationalistic belief that such ideas as an evil entity are archaic and out of place in modern, enlightened societies. Sadly this lie has permeated certain sections of the Church and I have met priests who do not believe in the existence of an evil spiritual being, but explain it away as merely psychological disturbance. Jesus himself however, frequently encountered the devil head on and set many people free who had been afflicted by the effects of evil. He even refers to this evil being by several names, including 'the prince of this world', and the 'Father of lies.' How anybody can dismiss this as simply 'Jesus working within the context of the limited under-standing of the people He was dealing with' as I heard one academic say, I just cannot understand.

No wonder the day we attended the F.G.B.M.F.I. dinner was fraught with difficulties and misunderstandings when we were up against such a powerful enemy, determined to prevent Warren from encountering Christ. Saint Paul in his letter to the Ephesians warns: "For our struggles are not against flesh and blood but against… the powers of this dark world and against the spiritual forces of evil in the heavenly realms." Warren and I began to read the bible and pray together and it was a time of rapid growth for us both. We committed our marriage to the Lord and handed over our future to Him and it wasn't long before the Lord put this to the test.

CHAPTER TWELVE

On the Move Again

Do not be afraid, for wherever you go,
the Lord your God goes with you
(Joshua 1: 9)

One evening, about a month later, Warren came home from work and without any preamble said: "How would you like to live in Great Yarmouth?" He had been asked to open a new office in Norfolk and was keen to take up the challenge. My immediate reaction was: "Oh No! I've had enough of moving around in the past. If this is what comes of handing our lives over to the Lord, maybe it wasn't such a good idea after all!" However, we decided to put our faith into action and trust the Lord and we set the wheels in motion. The first hurdle would be to sell our house.

"You couldn't have picked a worse time to sell your house! You must be mad!" We heard many such gloomy pronouncements on a daily basis because due to a downturn in the offshore oil industry, many people were selling up and leaving Aberdeen. As a result there was a glut of houses for sale and too few buyers. However, we didn't have much choice and trying to ignore the Job's comforters we put our house on the market. Before it had even been advertised in the local paper a couple who had spotted the 'For Sale' sign as they drove past, contacted us and after viewing, they immediately made us an offer which we accepted. We took this to be a 'go-ahead' from the Lord.

"Do you realise just how lucky you are to have sold your house just now?" We were asked this question many times: we preferred to call it providence rather than luck.

After tearful farewells to friends and family we set out on a cold snowy day in January 1986, with mixed feelings. I was sad to be leaving Scotland which I had grown to love but I was also excited at the prospect of a new life in Norfolk which I knew was a beautiful part of England. When we first arrived my heart sank; I thought we had made a terrible mistake.

Out of season seaside towns are not at their best in winter and Great Yarmouth was no exception. Walking around the almost empty streets and shops after the hustle and bustle of Aberdeen was a depressing experience and all that was missing was tumbleweed blowing through the deserted streets. However, once we found a suitable house we quickly settled in. We were welcomed into St. Mary's the local parish and I joined the prayer group where I soon made lasting friendships. Things brightened up when

Easter came and the first visitors began to trickle into town.

About a year after my conversion experience I hit a bad patch. With hindsight I see it as a time of growth but at the time it was very painful. Whereas previously I had found prayer to be a delightful experience and I loved reading the bible, all of a sudden I had little appetite for prayer and no desire to read the bible. It all seemed suddenly dry and lifeless and no matter how hard I tried I could no longer work up any enthusiasm. I couldn't even face going to Mass because I would just break down and cry for no apparent reason. A black cloud settled on me and for the next six months God seemed totally remote. Perhaps I had imagined everything that had happened in the previous year; maybe it was all just emotionalism after all? I never doubted my original experience of God's love, but I began to wish He'd left me alone if He was just going to abandon me now.

Gradually however, almost imperceptibly I emerged from the darkness and slowly my spiritual depression lifted. The lesson I learned from this dark time is that God is always with us, no matter what our feelings tell us and it was important for me to persevere and just hang on in there. Perhaps I had begun to depend too much on feeling good during prayer times and became discouraged when the 'feel good factor' deserted me. I believe it is possible to seek spiritual 'highs' and I think the Lord was teaching me to rely on faith more than feelings and to trust him more completely. I have experienced many spiritual deserts since that time and I feel they are times of growth, more so than when I have experienced consolation in prayer.

During our time in Great Yarmouth we had lots of friends and family visiting us during the summer months and I enjoyed playing the role of tour guide. One summer, Simon, who still lived in Aberdeen, spent a week with friends on the Broads in a cabin cruiser and they visited us when they tied up at Yarmouth. It was purely coincidental of course that their dirty washing had begun to mount up and the shower had broken down at the same time - not to mention the fact they were all starving and fast running out of money!

We spent three happy years in Yarmouth before Warren was transferred back to Aberdeen in May 1989. During our stay in Yarmouth we were very involved in AA and we had the privilege of seeing many people get sober in the fellowship. In addition to this, we also shared the gospel with those who expressed an interest and had the joy of seeing them commit their lives to Christ. Although we were sad to leave the good friends we had made in Norfolk, after much prayer, we believed that the time was now right to move back to Scotland.

We bought a new house in the same parish we had lived in previously and quickly settled back down to life in Aberdeen. I was delighted when in October 1990 Simon's wife Cheryl presented us with our first grandchild Joshua. I was thrilled as I held him in my arms but my joy was tinged with sorrow as I thought about the baby I had given up for adoption so long ago. I could only imagine how horrified Cheryl would be at the thought of having to hand her beautiful little baby over to strangers, never to be seen again. I tried to suppress my sorrow, but it was never far from the surface.

"It's that time of year again isn't it?" It was the month of November and apart from the gloomy winter weather, it was the time of year when painful memories surfaced.   I remembered the months I'd spent in Brettargh Holt and the joy I'd felt when I had held my baby in my arms for the first time. The joy was short lived while the pain went on and on. It would soon be my daughter's twenty-fifth birthday and I didn't even know if she was alive or dead. I tried not to torment myself with vain imaginings but it was hard not to sit and wonder where she was and what she was doing. I asked myself is she married and does she have children? Perhaps I had grandchildren who would never know me. I worried that she might think I'd given her away because I simply hadn't wanted her.

Society had changed so much since 1964; nowadays there is help available for single mothers and it would be hard for my daughter to imagine the social climate which existed back in the Sixties and the stigma which was attached to illegitimacy. I had so many unanswered questions and no means of answering them because the natural mother has no legal rights to access the adoption records. Friends who knew my secret asked why I had not tried to find my daughter: they didn't realise it was not possible. The law forbade access to any information which might lead to a woman tracing a child given up for adoption. I believe the law might change with regard to this and in future, birth mothers may be able to trace their children.

If only my daughter knew how much I had fought to keep her and how miserable I was when I had to give her up. It hurt me deeply to think she might feel that I had abandoned her but my hands were tied.   It was a strain keeping this secret from the other children. Many times I had been on the verge of telling the older children about her but I was afraid it would unsettle them, knowing that somewhere 'out there' they had a sister they would never meet. I felt especially sad for Sara as I knew she'd always longed to have a sister. I wondered what my daughter looked like and whether I would recognise her if I passed her on the street. Such thoughts tormented me but there was nothing I could do about it. Although I bravely tried to hand it all over to God, the questions remained and I could only hope and pray that she was safe and well and that she had found happiness.

There have been several significant people in my life who have turned up at just the right moment and Sister Josephine Walsh, DHG (Daughter of the Holy Ghost) is one such person. She is one of the liveliest people I know, and one of most positive and if she makes a promise she will see it through.

I first met Sister Josephine in Gorleston when she led a day of healing and renewal. At that time I was struggling to stop smoking and was in the throes of yet another bout of bronchitis; I decided I had nothing to lose by going along to the healing session. Whenever healing is mentioned people usually presume this refers to physical healing but this is only one aspect of it. In fact many people are healed of inner conflicts, fears and psychological problems which have blighted their lives for years. Whilst I went along hoping for healing of my bronchitis and the strength to quit smoking, I believe God had other ideas.

After giving her talk, Sister Josephine asked us to form small groups of four or five and then encouraged us to pray for each other. At one point she joined the group I was in and immediately homed in on me. She laid her hands on me and began to pray quietly. Apparently God had given her an insight, often referred to as a 'word of knowledge', regarding certain aspects of my life, including the fact that my Dad had died when I was a child and that I'd grown up feeling unloved and unwanted. I was astonished when she told me this and a little afraid. How could a total stranger have such knowledge? At the time it spooked me a bit as I didn't know much about the Gifts of the Holy Spirit and how they operated.

As Sister Josephine prayed with me, many painful memories from my childhood came flooding back and I began to sob uncontrollably. I thought I would never stop crying but when the flood subsided, a deep sense of peace descended and I felt as though the Lord Himself were cradling me in His arms. This was the first of many such healings, and over a period of years the Lord has dealt with other hurts from my past which had been affecting me. I went home that day still addicted to cigarettes but with a much lighter heart! When the time was right, the Lord would set me free from my addiction to nicotine but in the meantime there were other problems He wanted to deal with and that day was the beginning of a gradual healing of a profound sense of rejection I had borne since childhood.

I was to meet Sr. Josephine many times over the next few years and I remember one particular occasion when I travelled with her to Medjugorge. One day whilst we were enjoying lunch in a local restaurant, we were talking about the aftermath of the war and the terrible suffering endured by thousands of people who were now homeless. A United Nations soldier sitting nearby told Sr. Josephine that there were refugees in the vicinity of Medjugorge and in fact there was a camp close by. We looked at our empty plates and thought about the delicious meal we had just enjoyed. It was terrible to think that close by, there were people who had lost their homes and didn't know where their next meal was coming from. Deciding there and then to see for ourselves, a group of us took a taxi to the camp and were appalled at what we found. The people were so poor it was heartbreaking.

The camp consisted mainly of women and children with a few elderly men living in dilapidated old railway carriages. Many of the young men had been involved in the conflict and their families didn't know whether they were dead or alive as they had been driven out of their villages as a result of the so-called 'ethnic cleansing.' There were so many displaced persons that it was almost impossible for their families to trace them. The basic amenities such as decent toilets and showers were lacking and the people had no warm clothing or proper footwear. Most of the refugees wore only flimsy sandals and were dreading the onset of winter.

On the way out to the camp we spotted a small village shop which, much to our surprise had several boxes of bananas sitting outside. Sr. Josephine ordered the taxi driver to stop at once and we bought a whole crate of bananas. These poor refugees had not tasted a banana since the war broke out four years previously and it was humbling to see how grateful they were for such a small gift although it was distressing to see how they pushed and shoved each other in the scrabble to get a banana. Fear and desperation had robbed many of them of their human dignity. However, despite their dire poverty we were invited to join them in their railway carriage homes where they offered us glasses of juice. What little they had, they wanted to share with their visitors.

We were horrified at the squalid conditions they were living in and we knew that because of the political situation, they would never be able to return to their former homes. Sister Josephine promised to return to the camp and bring essential supplies to them. I don't suppose they believed her but two months later she was standing at the gates once more, this time with a container load of warm clothing and new footwear as well as small gifts such as mirrors, cosmetics and toiletries which the ladies greatly appreciated.

Once more Sister Josephine demonstrated the power of love and prayer as God provided everything that was needed through generous donors, including the transport necessary to take the goods to these needy people. In addition, Sister Josephine had alerted the International Red Cross to conditions in the camp and new shower blocks and toilets were soon installed. She has since gone on to found Housing Aid Bosnia and has achieved amazing results in placing many of the refugee families in beautiful new homes where they can raise their own produce and even keep a cow and a few chickens. Their dignity restored, they have gone on to get married, raise new families and become a credit to their community and a testimony to the resilience of the human spirit. Sr. Josephine's dedicated work with the refugees continues to this day and she is determined that every family will eventually have a decent home of their own.

From time to time Sister Josephine was invited to Aberdeen where she led weekends entitled 'Healing and Wholeness in Jesus Christ' and during one such weekend in 1993 she prayed with me for the healing of memories. It was the 20th November, and my daughter whom I had not seen since that cold January day when I had handed her over to strangers, would be celebrating her twenty-ninth birthday. I tried to imagine her as she was now; no longer a child but a full grown woman who may have children of her own. What was going through her mind right now? Did she spare a thought for me and wonder where I was? My heart ached and I longed to know where she was and how life had treated her. I wept bitterly as Sister Josephine laid hands on me and prayed a very brief prayer. "Jesus" she said, "you know all things, and you know where Margaret's daughter is right now. She's waited twenty-nine years Lord so please bring them back together again. Thank you Lord. Amen!"

I must confess I thought it was a pretty hopeless prayer. I still believed that I had no right to ask God for this miracle as He had done so much for me already but I thought it best to humour Sister Josephine! If I was honest, I was afraid my daughter would not want anything to do with me because although it wasn't possible for me to trace my child, she would have been entitled to access her birth details once she reached the age of eighteen. Surely, I reasoned, if she had wanted to trace me she would have done so by now. My thoughts were in turmoil as I lay in my bed that night. But one thing was certain I daren't place too much hope in Sr. Josephine's prayer.

CHAPTER THIRTEEN

Together Again

Can a mother forget her baby?
Or a woman the child of her womb?
(Isaiah. 49: 15)

Christmas was fast approaching and I was soon caught up in all the usual preparations. With shopping to do, gifts to wrap and cards to write I soon forgot all about Sr. Josephine's prayer. I hurried home from mass one Sunday morning just before Christmas determined to finish off some last minute gift wrapping. I had hardly got in the front door when the phone rang.

"If that's for me could you tell them I'll call them back. I really must finish wrapping these gifts." But Warren handed me the phone with a shrug; "It's Sheila and she insists on speaking to you; says it's urgent!" My heart sank. "Oh. No. Not bad news?"

My sister sounded excited. "Where have you been?" she said. "I've been trying to phone you since last night. I've got some amazing news for you!" As it happens we'd been out for dinner the previous evening and apparently the baby-sitter had forgotten to pass on Sheila's message asking me to phone her.

My heart began to race. "Are you sitting down?" she said. "I've got something to tell you and it's going to come as a bit of a shock. But don't worry" she added, "it's good news!" I could sense her excitement and I sat down in a state of shock. I suddenly knew what she was going to tell me. "My daughter's traced me!" I yelled.

"How did you know?" Sheila was amazed. How could I have possibly guessed? I couldn't explain it but somehow I just knew. Sheila continued: "She's going to phone you this morning so I thought I'd better warn you." I was so overcome with emotion I could hardly speak. After nearly thirty years I was going to speak to my daughter. I was in such a state of shock I was shaking like a leaf. I felt light headed and sick with nerves. "What if she doesn't like me?" I thought. All the old negative thinking surfaced.

I could hardly contain my excitement as I waited for the phone to ring and when I lifted the receiver my hands were shaking and my mouth was dry. A warm cheery voice said "Hi Margaret? This is Helen." At first I was confused; after all, my daughter's name was Kathryn. She went on to explain that her adoptive parents had already adopted a little girl called Catherine and so they had re-named my baby Helen. There were lots of tears at first and long silences whilst we tried to compose ourselves. How do you catch up with twenty-nine lost years in one telephone conversation? We spent the next hour and a half filling in some of the blanks.

"What colour is your hair; your eyes? How tall are you?" she said. When I replied: "Five foot nothing," she laughed and said "Oh that explains my short legs!" She was very easy to speak to and I soon felt completely at ease.

"Do I by any chance have Irish blood?" she said. "Yes, you do actually." I replied. "My grandmother was Irish, although she was born in Calcutta as her Dad was serving in the army. The family are from Enniskillen." Helen said that people often asked her if she was Irish. "It's like fitting together the missing pieces of a jigsaw puzzle. I'm dying to meet you!"

We agreed she should come up to Aberdeen in the New Year and in the meantime we spoke to each other daily on the phone and exchanged photographs. When I finally saw a photo of her, I was struck by the strong resemblance to myself when I was young.

Christmas came and went in a blur and as the day when Helen was due to arrive drew closer, I became increasingly anxious. I was so afraid she would be disappointed in me, she wouldn't like me or she would be angry with me. It was not easy telling the other children about Helen. Naturally they were shocked at first and surprised to know that I had kept this secret for so long. Before long though, natural curiosity soon overcame any fears they had and they were as excited as me about the prospect of meeting their new sister.

On the second of January 1994, I opened the door to be faced with a mirror image of myself when I was young. Although we had exchanged photos, nothing could have prepared us for the shock of seeing each other face to face. The likeness was startling and we spent the first couple of hours staring shyly at each other. We share many of the same mannerisms and both of us use our hands a lot when we are speaking. Warren was shocked when he saw us together. "I can't believe there's another one like you Margaret!" he laughed.

That first day Helen and I walked for hours in the local park. We both had so many questions. "Why did you wait so long to trace me?" I asked. "You could have started looking for me when you were eighteen."

"Well, actually I did try" she said. "It was just after my eighteenth birthday but the social worker I discussed it with warned me that sometimes women who'd given a baby up for adoption were afraid it would cause too much disruption in their family and preferred to let sleeping dogs lie. She asked me if I was willing to take the chance that you might not want to see me and of course I said no. The thought of being rejected by you was too painful. It would have been worse than not finding you."

"So why did you change your mind after all this time?" I said. "Well actually, it was on my birthday when I suddenly decided that I was going to try to find you. I wanted to see my natural mother at least once in my life and if you shut the door in my face, well, that was a risk I just had to take."

"How amazing!" I said. "That was the day that Sister Josephine prayed for us to be reunited!" I told Helen about the day of healing and the special prayer I'd received and admitted that I had not held out much hope of it being answered.

"Well," she said smiling, "I guess it worked because I suddenly knew I just had to find you! I suppose it was because it was my birthday because every year I'd wonder if you were thinking about me on that day."

"Helen" I said, "not a day has gone by since you were born when I haven't thought about you and wondered where you were and whether you were happy. Sometimes I just longed to know whether you were still alive." Only somebody who has experienced this can appreciate the pain of a mother being separated from her child against her will. Many people thought you didn't deserve any sympathy, after all you had 'brought it upon yourself' and so 'it served you right.'

Although Helen had spent a very happy childhood on a farm and her adoptive parents were good, kind people, she always wondered who her natural parents were and as her adoptive mother refused point blank to discuss her adoption, she'd had to live with many unanswered questions. The first and most important question for her was: 'Why?' 'Why had she been given up for adoption?'

'Why had I not kept her?' 'Did I simply not want her?'

She told me that since her early teens these questions had tormented her. The thought of her own mother rejecting her was unbearable. It was hard for her to understand just how different things were back in 1964 and how attitudes have changed so drastically since then.

There were other aspects of being adopted which had proved problematic, such as the question of the family's medical history. For instance, when Helen was seven years old a small mole on her face had turned out to be malignant and she had received treatment which thankfully completely cured it. During this worrying time all sorts of questions had arisen regarding her medical history. The doctors had to proceed pretty much in the dark. These questions had planted seeds of anxiety in Helen. In addition, although her adoptive family was kind, Helen had always felt like the 'odd one out'.

"I just felt that I didn't really fit in," she said. "I just knew I wasn't one of them. When I discovered I was adopted, at last I understood why I felt this way."

When Helen eventually met other members of my family such as uncles and aunts, she could see many of her own character traits mirrored in them. We tend to have a rather zany sense of humour in our family, not always appreciated by others; but Helen shares this same sense of humour and fitted in with our family immediately. "Now I know why I'm a little crazy!" she laughed.

Another poignant moment came when we finally visited the cemetery in Barrow where we stood in silence at my parent's grave. "You don't know what it means to me to finally know where I came from and where my roots are." We held each other as we looked out to sea and thought about how different things could have been if only I could have kept her. It would take a long time to catch up with each other's lives but we had the rest of our lives now to make up for lost time – although, of course, nothing could replace the twenty-nine years we'd spent apart.

Helen had been preoccupied from an early age with finding out just who her 'real mother' was and I wept as she told me of the many occasions when she'd been in a crowd and wondered; "Could that be my mother?" when she thought she spotted a resemblance in a passer-by.

Shortly before her eighteenth birthday, Helen had taken a seasonal job in Jersey. One night as she walked on the beach with friends she suddenly felt overwhelmed with sadness as she looked at them laughing and joking together. They all knew who their parents and grandparents were. "But who am I and where do I come from?" she thought. "Do I have brothers and sisters, aunts, uncles and cousins? The whole network of family that most people take for granted was totally lost to me. I felt desolate that night and totally abandoned" she said as we sat on the park bench.

"Standing on that beach in Jersey, I looked out to sea and shouted: 'Where are you? I need you!'" How could she know that at the opposite end of the country I was asking the same question?

She went on: "I was put off by stories I heard about people who'd met their natural mothers and found that they either had nothing in common or didn't even like each other. I felt vulnerable enough as it was. I couldn't risk your refusing to meet me so I tried to forget about you." Of course, it was just as impossible for Helen to forget about me as it was for me to forget about her. Her insecurity had affected her relationship with her husband David and together they'd sought the help of a counsellor.

"You'll never have peace of mind unless you at least try to find your natural mother. I believe that's what's causing your problems," the counsellor had said. "You need to find your roots, whatever the truth is. It will be less painful in the long term than tormenting yourself with so many unanswered questions. It is better to face the truth than spend your life being tormented by your imagination."

Finally, on her twenty-ninth birthday, Helen reached a decision. "I'm going to find my mother if it's the last thing I do" she told her husband. "Whatever I find, it surely can't be worse than this uncertainty. It's destroying me." Naturally David was concerned, as he was afraid Helen might be even more hurt if she managed to track her mother down and was rejected, but he agreed to support her in the search. Once this decision had been reached, Social Services set the wheels in motion to enable Helen to begin the search.

"I have never known a case with so much information on file," said the Social Worker when she finally brought Helen the details she needed. In addition to the birth certificate there was a letter on file which I had written in desperation to the adoption society. In the letter I wrote how much I loved this baby and didn't want to give her up but I had no choice. It was obvious from the letter that I didn't want to go through with the adoption and when Helen read it twenty-nine years later, she was overjoyed to know that at least she'd been loved and wanted when she was born but circumstances meant I couldn't keep her. She now had my maiden name and former address, the next step was to get hold of a telephone directory for Barrow. It just so happened that the first person in the directory with the same surname was my oldest brother Alf.

Tactfully, Helen didn't immediately reveal who she was, as she was afraid my family might not even know that I'd had a baby as she knew that many girls had hidden their pregnancies and had gone off to mother and baby homes without their family knowing anything about it. After confirming that I was indeed his sister, Helen told Alf that she was trying to organise a school reunion and wanted to contact me and he suggested she speak to my sister Sheila. When Helen spoke to my sister, after a few tentative enquiries, she asked Sheila outright if her sister Margaret had had a baby in November 1964 which she'd given up for adoption. Sheila was initially shocked when she realised who it was she was speaking to. But she quickly assured Helen that she need not be afraid to phone me as she knew it was an answer to prayer.

"Do you think she will want to meet me?" Helen asked, rather nervously. Sheila laughed; "Well you need have no fears on that score. If only you knew how much Margaret's longed to see you all these years? Never a day goes by

without her thinking of you. She was so afraid that you
might not even be alive. She had no way of finding out
anything about you. I just wish I could be there when you
meet her!"

Now that we were face to face I tried to answer Helen's
questions as honestly as I could. She was relieved to know
she had been deeply loved and wanted and that I'd had no
choice when I gave her up for adoption. The years fell away
as we walked and talked throughout that first day. I must
say we are very blessed in that there was an instant rapport
between us.

Unfortunately this is not always the case and I have read
sad stories of people who have been bitterly   disappointed
when they eventually met their natural mother. That's not
to say that our relationship has not had its ups and downs
and there were moments when her anger spilled over. I
knew that this was not a fairy tale with a happy ever after
ending and that it would take time to reconnect with my
child and renew the shattered bond. You can't just tear
something apart and expect it to be renewed instantly.
There was one thing in particular that Helen wanted to
do and I knew that it would be very painful for us both. I
didn't know if I could handle it, but for her sake I decided
to try. Helen wanted to visit the place where she was born.

"Will you come with me to Brettargh Holt?" I need to see
where I was born and it's important that you're with me."
"I don't know if I can face it Helen, but if you really want
to go there, I'll come with you".

I had mixed feelings about going back to the place which held such painful memories for me, but if this was something Helen felt she must do then I would try to put my own feelings aside. In these days of abortion on demand, very few mother and baby homes remain and Brettargh Holt is no longer used for this purpose. Nowadays it is a popular venue for retreats and conferences, set as it is in the beautiful English Lake District.

"Is this the place?" David asked as we approached the imposing entrance. "Yes." I said dully. "Could you just wait a moment please?" As I gazed down the sweeping drive and caught a glimpse of the gracious old house, my heart began to race and I felt light headed. I wasn't sure I could handle this but for the sake of Helen I would try. Breathing a quick prayer, I told David I was as ready as I'd ever be and we turned into the tree lined drive.

As we approached the house I caught sight of the very window where I had stood and watched as strangers drove off with my baby and I was suddenly overwhelmed with sadness. As we drew up at the front door, I was shaking and would have fled if Helen hadn't been gripping my hand. I could only hope this wouldn't turn out to be a terrible mistake. "Come on Margaret" she said. "We're in this together. I know it can't be easy for you, but it's something I just have to do and I can't do it without you."

It was the same heavy oak door that had closed firmly behind me all those years ago when I'd trudged up the drive after Helen had been taken away. Clutching a battered case, I had nothing to show for the nine months I'd carried my child and the brief time when I'd been able to give her my love. Painful memories flooded back and I broke down and wept before we even rang the doorbell. Footsteps sounded on the parquet floor and the door swung open to reveal the same hallway which had hardly changed in all those years: the shiny parquet floor which we girls had sweated over, the same old clock ticking ponderously in the corner - and the same grand staircase which we'd swept on our hands and knees.

"Welcome my dears come along in." A diminutive figure dressed in a modern habit with short veil and knee length skirt, smiled kindly as she showed us into the parlour. How different she looks, I thought, as I remembered the old fashioned habits which the sisters wore when I'd been there. Their long black garments had swept the floor and their wimples obscured most of their faces making them look rather strange and intimidating. She introduced herself as Sr. Martha and glancing briefly at my tear stained face, she gently laid a hand upon my arm. "Come along my dear" she said kindly as she ushered us into the parlour. She was not surprised by our request to have a look around and she told us that they are often visited by people who were born there, although it was not so common for a mother and child to come together.

"Sadly not every story has a happy ending like yours," she said as she poured tea into delicate china cups. She told us of instances where the natural mother had been afraid to acknowledge the child. This was often because they had since got married and felt too ashamed to tell their husbands about the baby they had given up for adoption. I was grateful I had never had that problem, having told both David and Warren all about my first born child.

Sister Martha recalled one case in particular when a girl had travelled to Brettargh Holt all the way from Australia, having emigrated with her adoptive parents when she was just six years old. She travelled all the way back to England to meet her natural mother but sadly when they met, she had received a chilly reception. Her mother had insisted that it was better to leave the past alone and had wanted no further contact with her. Apparently the broken-hearted girl had made the sad journey to Brettargh Holt alone. If she couldn't meet her mother, at least she could see the place where she was born.

As we walked around the old house, Helen and I were lost in our own thoughts. Apart from the entrance hall which had remained pretty much the same there were quite a few changes to the place as it had been adapted for its new purpose. But it was familiar enough to cause a stab of pain as I gazed out of the window of what had once been the nursery and the years just rolled away. In my minds eye I could see myself holding that beautiful little baby whom I would soon have to hand over to total strangers. I relived the anguish as I walked silently around the once familiar rooms.

When we reached the chapel where I had spent so many hours begging God to let me keep my baby, I broke down and wept bitterly. I longed for Helen to take hold of me and comfort me but it was David, her husband, who consoled me. She told me later she that at that moment she'd felt very angry with me and wanted to punish me.

"Serves her right!" she thought bitterly. "How could she have given me away? What kind of mother gives her child away?" This is the most painful aspect for me, the fact that Helen can't really understand how impossible it was for me to keep her and I think there is still an element of anger there. However, I can only pray that the Lord will bring peace and healing in due course and that Helen will understand finally that I really had no choice.

As we left Brettargh Holt that day, I reflected that at least this time we were leaving together and that nobody would ever separate us again. Although Helen and I hit it off immediately, we have had our difficult moments and it was naive to imagine that those missing years could be glossed over without painful feelings surfacing. It's not easy in our current social climate to imagine what it was like forty years ago and how unmarried mothers were ostracised and treated like criminals. We were sent off to homes in the wilds of the country and left in no doubt that we deserved to be punished for our wickedness. We even lost our identity in a sense when they gave us fictitious names.

Many sad tales have emerged in the years since the large mental hospitals were closed of women who were incarcerated in these institutions for no other reason than that they had an illegitimate child. In today's permissive climate it's almost unbelievable and I can understand Helen's bitterness but I too paid a terrible price and nothing can replace those lost years for either of us. Others tell horror stories of cruelty meted out to them in the

'Magdalene Laundries' in Ireland. Thankfully at least the sisters were kind to us in Brettargh Holt and did their best for us in difficult circumstances.

The first time I went to stay at Helen's home we had a blazing row which in fact was another step forward in the healing process. Helen was very resentful that she'd been 'given away' as she put it. I had been listing all the benefits she had during her childhood such as living on a farm and having a pony, things which I could never have given her. She rounded on me angrily. "Never mind ponies!" she stormed, "I should have been with my own mother, not given away to strangers!" She turned her back on me and gazed angrily at the rain lashed street.

"Helen. You don't understand, there was no help for unmarried mothers in those days. If your family wouldn't help, then adoption was the only solution. There were no State Benefits available for unmarried mothers. Unless you had somebody to take care of the baby whilst you went out to work, it was hopeless. You didn't get a penny from the State, never mind a flat and a weekly allowance! As far as society was concerned in those days, you had done wrong and deserved to be punished. It was a case of 'You made your bed now lie on it!' It was as simple as that. People didn't have multiple partners and babies to umpteen different men! Society now accepts this behaviour, that's why it's so difficult for you to grasp how drastically different it was back then! Yes, I did wrong, but I paid dearly for it for nearly thirty years; we both did. I am sorry Helen, but I can't turn the clock back."

There was an awkward silence and it seemed an age before she finally turned round with tears coursing down her cheeks. "I'm sorry" she said. "I just feel so cheated. All these years when I never even knew you and nothing will bring them back."

Although I understood her pain, it was hurtful to think she believed it I had given her away lightly. However, I am glad she felt able to be honest with me. That's a characteristic we share, frankness. I can't stand pussyfooting around and tend to call a spade a spade! At least it cleared the air between us and we ended up clinging to each other in tears. In fact, she sat on my knee and wept. "I've waited all my life for this moment," she said. "To sit on my mother's lap!" She still calls me Margaret rather than 'Mum,' which is only natural. I wouldn't expect her to do otherwise. The first card she sent me on Mothers' Day was a very pretty card but didn't mention the word 'Mother'. However the following year she sent me a beautiful bouquet of flowers and a card inscribed: "To a Wonderful Mum" and she's done so every year since.

Helen's adopted sister seems to have been largely unaffected by the fact that she was adopted. Unlike Helen, she has shown little curiosity regarding her natural mother and has no desire to find her. Helen said she felt cheated of her natural family, and when she found us she knew that at last she had 'come home.' For our part she was so obviously 'one of us' that any initial shyness soon melted away.

Helen had a wonderful upbringing and I am so grateful for

that. I could never replace the woman who has truly been a Mother to her for all these years, nor would I wish to. I have no desire to interfere with her relationship with Helen in any way but I am deeply saddened by the fact that she refuses to acknowledge my existence. I have tried to see it from her point of view. Perhaps she sees me as a threat?

Helen was so afraid of upsetting her adoptive Mum that she didn't tell her that she had traced me. This went on for many years until finally, unable to continue with the deception any longer, Helen told her mother that she had found me and had been in contact with me and her newly-found brothers and sister for the past fourteen years. Apparently her Mum has never been willing to even discuss the fact that Helen is adopted, and refuses point blank to talk about the circumstances of her adoption. Helen once asked her how she'd feel if she tried to find her natural mother and her Mum was furious. I suppose it's a sign of insecurity and a fear that if Helen traced her natural mother, this stranger would replace her in Helen's affections which is, of course, impossible. Having finally told her Mum the truth, sadly, her Mum is unable to see it from Helen's point of view and flatly refuses to discuss it further. She has forbidden Helen to mention me ever again. I feel sad because if she only knew how grateful I am to her and that I have no desire to come between them, she would realise that her fears are quite unfounded and we could have even become friends. However there is nothing I can do and I can only pray for her and place the situation in the Lord's hands.

CHAPTER FOURTEEN

Lightning Does Strike Twice!

All the days ordained for me
were written in your book
before one of them came to be
(Psalms 139: 16)

Before she traced me, Helen had been hoping to have children for several years with no success but since meeting me she has gone on to have two lovely children, Michael and Megan. She wonders if there was some psychological blockage preventing her from conceiving. Only the good Lord knows the truth of that. Unfortunately, the children don't know who I really am and think that I am just one of their Mum's friends. It was a poignant moment for me when I went to stay with Helen and was unpacking my things in Megan's room. Michael said solemnly, "Margaret, this spare bed is grandma's when she stays here, but you can use it while you're here." I had to turn away quickly as

I tried to hide my tears from this dear little child who has no idea who I really am. One day, no doubt, the truth will come out and I just hope I live long enough to see that day.

Already Michael has noticed the remarkable resemblance between his mother and me and after visiting my home he remarked: "Mum, I didn't know you'd been to India?" When Helen assured him that she had never been there, he replied: "Yes, you have! I saw a photo of you in India in Margaret's house." It was of course a photo of me taken at the Taj Mahal, and Helen tried to brush it aside by saying that there are lots of people in the world who look alike and hastily changed the subject.

After sharing my sadness for so many years, Warren was thrilled to be able to share my joy. He was a wonderful Dad to Simon and Sara, as well as his own two boys and now he opened his heart to this long lost child of mine. As a typical gesture of his generosity, a few months after our first meeting Warren arranged for us to meet up with Helen and David in Glasgow so we could spend the weekend together.

It was late April and the weather was glorious. On the Saturday afternoon Warren and David went to a football match whilst Helen and I spent the afternoon shopping and chatting - we had a lot of catching up to do! That evening we went out with some friends for a meal and on Sunday we took some final snapshots before parting company amid much laughter. We felt we had all drawn closer to each other during those few precious days.

As she was leaving, Helen said to Warren, "Now you take good care of her. I've just found her and I don't want to lose her!" Warren laughed saying: "Don't worry Helen. I've always looked after her and I always will!" Helen was referring to my forthcoming surgery, as I was scheduled to have a hysterectomy.

On the journey home Warren and I chatted about the weekend, agreeing it had been a very special time. Although he was tired Warren insisted on driving. We stopped off for a coffee at our favourite café and I noticed how weary he seemed, but after two very late nights and a packed weekend, we were both pretty exhausted so I didn't attach too much importance to it.

Warren had to travel back to Glasgow on business two days later and he left the house early without waking me. Later that morning whilst walking the dog in the nearby forest, I had a rather unusual experience. I suddenly felt a strong, comforting presence all around me: it was almost tangible. In fact I can best describe it as a feeling of being wrapped in a warm blanket, surrounded by angels! It only lasted for a few moments but the effect lasted all day. Still puzzled by this experience, I showered and changed when I got home as I was joining friends for a birthday celebration later that day. As I stepped out of the shower the phone rang. I normally let the answering machine pick up calls when I'm showering but for some reason that morning I had taken the phone into the bathroom with me and I was glad, because it was Warren calling me from his car phone. I teased him about missing my morning cup of tea which he usually brought me before he left for work.

"You looked so peaceful," he said "and you know what they
say about sleeping dogs...?" We chatted for a little while
longer and he said he would call me that evening to let me
know which hotel the company had booked him into. His
last words to me were: "I love you." "And I love you too!"
I replied. "Have a good day. I'll speak to you tonight. Take
care and drive safely!" As I quickly got ready to meet my
friends, I reflected on how lucky I was to have met Warren
and what a kind and loving husband he was.

As I drove along Deeside that day, I watched the lambs
frisking in the fields and marvelled at the beauty of the
banks of daffodils which covered the hills. I love springtime
with its new life and promise of things to come and as it was
almost May, the countryside looked quite spectacular. It
was my friend's birthday and several of us joined her for
lunch. We had a lovely day and there was much laughter
when I told my friends about the rather strange experience
I'd had that morning whilst walking the dog.

"I know it sounds weird, but it felt like there were angels all
around me!" I don't know what my friends were thinking,
but there was much good natured teasing about eating
too much cheese at bedtime! I'm sure they thought I was
imagining things and I didn't blame them in the least, after
all it did sound a bit fanciful.

After spending a wonderful day with my friends, I drove
home happily singing along to praise songs and enjoying
the late afternoon sun. I collected the boys from Simon's
house and hurried home to prepare supper. The boys and I
had just settled down to eat and I was telling them all about

my lovely day when the phone rang.

"It never fails! As soon as we sit down to eat, the phone rings!" I said resignedly. It was Warren's boss Ian and I was surprised as I knew they had planned to go for a game of golf after work. Ian interrupted my cheerful greeting.

"Margaret, I'm afraid I have some terrible news about Warren." I suddenly felt sick; I was gripped by a sense of foreboding. "Oh No! He's not... !" I cried. I didn't even finish the sentence. "I'm afraid he is," said Ian and I knew instinctively that Warren was dead. I heard myself shouting, "No Lord! Please, not again!"

Ian went on to say how they had gone for a round of golf as planned and Warren was in good spirits. Just as he teed off at the first hole, without any warning Warren collapsed. It was as sudden as that; he had suffered a massive heart attack and death was almost instantaneous. Some paramedics who just happened to be close by rushed to Warren's aid and tried desperately to revive him but despite their best efforts it was too late.

Numbness set in and I went into shock. I tried to get hold of Simon on the phone but his line was engaged. Unfortunately just when I needed him most, his phone had accidentally been knocked off the hook. As he lived just around the corner from us, in sheer desperation I sent Michael round on his bike to tell Simon what had happened.

When I look back, I'm horrified. How could I have sent a

child to tell his brother such terrible news? But shock often makes people do strange things, for instance whilst I was waiting for Simon to arrive I went out to the garden in a daze to fetch the washing in and I even started to fold it and put it away. I was gripped by a strange, detached feeling and everything felt totally unreal.

Simon arrived looking ashen. He said "Mum, I can't believe it; I've lost two Dads now." That was when I collapsed in tears. Simon was a tower of strength for us all and I was especially grateful when he offered to make the heartbreaking journey to Glasgow to identify Warren. I simply couldn't face it but it had to be done.

There are many practical issues to be dealt with when there's a death in the family and for the next few days I felt like a detached observer, going through the motions. Surely it was all happening to somebody else?

The day after Warren died, after a sleepless night I had to go and meet an official from the local council at the cemetery to choose a burial plot. It was surreal; standing in the spring sunshine discussing the merits of various burial plots with an official wielding a clipboard, as though I were choosing a pair of shoes. Thankfully my friends Helen and Jamus Smith accompanied me; I simply could not have faced this alone.

Our parish priest, Father Myles, who had blessed our marriage in a very joyful ceremony, would now be performing a very different kind of service and he came to the house to discuss the funeral arrangements. I was deeply appreciative when he offered to pray with me and read words of comfort from the psalms. It would be some time before the full force of grief hit me. I felt as though a heavy weight was pressing down on me and at times it seemed as though I was actually suffocating.

One morning whilst in the shower, I was overcome by grief and from somewhere deep within cried out over and over again: "Abba!" the intimate name Jesus used to address His Father. Later that morning, the words of the Magnificat welled up from somewhere deep within: "My soul magnifies the Lord, and my Spirit rejoices in God my saviour." I was astonished; how could such joyful words spring to mind at one of the worst moments of my life?

Simon was a great comfort to Michael and Tony too as he could identify with their bewilderment, having lost his own father at roughly the same age as they were now. They were just ten and eleven years old. How could I expect them to accept that their Dad, with whom they'd been playing football the previous night, would never come home again?

"But why Mum? Why?" they asked me. "It's not fair!" As I looked at their anguished little faces I had no answers. I couldn't offer them pious platitudes or tell them "It's God's will." How could I expect two little boys to accept that? It was difficult enough for me. I didn't want them to blame God or become bitter. "No, boys it's not fair. Life is some-times very unfair" was all I could say.

I wasn't sure whether to let Michael and Tony see Warren

when he was taken to the funeral home but Simon thought we ought to let at least give them the choice. Simon said he'd always regretted not seeing his Dad when he died as it had made it more difficult for him to accept that his father really was dead. We made it clear to the boys that there was no pressure on them to go and see their Dad if they didn't want to but they both chose to go and see him and it was the right decision; it helped them accept the reality of his death.

I remembered when my own Dad had died, how everybody had tried to pretend that nothing had happened, brushing off my questions; I was determined not to make the same mistakes with my children. It was almost unbelievable; this was the second time I'd had to console bereaved children and I was no better prepared for it the second time around.

When my Dad died, well-intentioned people had tried to hide it from me and it actually made things worse. I was utterly bewildered and couldn't understand why my Dad had just disappeared without a word. Deep down I thought I must have done something very bad, that somehow I was responsible for his leaving. Apparently this is a common reaction from children. I think they are probably better able to deal with the truth than we give them credit for. But I had not been allowed to grieve as a child and my grief eventually surfaced in a destructive manner at a later date. We can't avoid pain, merely postpone it, and it seems the longer it is held at bay, the more destructive it can be. I learned at an early age to bury my pain and when I grew up, I used alcohol as an escape route.

"He's not there is he Mum?" said Michael when he got back from the funeral home. "Dad's gone hasn't he? It looks like him but somehow he's different." As young as he was, Michael sensed that the unique essence of his Dad was no longer there. "Yes Mike," I said. "Dad's soul has gone to heaven. That's why he seems so different."

My friend Helen Smith, who had taken me to my first healing service all those years ago, spent the first two nights with me until my family could travel up from England and her quiet presence was a great comfort to me. She didn't offer pious platitudes but said: "I can't even begin to imagine Margaret, what you are going through." Helen helped in very practical ways, making up beds for the visitors who were due to arrive as well as preparing a meal for them and seeing to whatever needed to be done around the house. It is at such times that one really values family and friends and I was completely overwhelmed by the love and kindness shown to us and the help we received was greatly appreciated.

We received dozens of letters and cards expressing condolences and support and many people who had dealings with Warren during the course of his working life wrote testifying to his impact on their lives. The word which occurred most frequently in these letters was integrity and I was deeply touched that these busy people with their high pressured jobs took the trouble to write to me.

Sometimes people hesitate to send a card or a letter to a bereaved person fearing they may not have the right words.

From my own experience, I would say go ahead and send it as it is immensely comforting just to know that others are thinking of you. In our culture we fear death and avoid talking about it as much as possible. In these supposedly enlightened times when many taboos have been swept away, the most ridiculous euphemisms are used for death. The most bizarre one I have heard to date was used in respect of the late Elvis Presley whose death was referred to in a magazine as his 'terminal event!' Many people even refused to accept that Elvis is dead and there have been numerous supposed 'sightings' of him. We just don't like to think about or talk about death – perhaps it reminds us of our own mortality. Unfortunately, due to the number of bereavements I suffered at an early age, I need no reminders of my own mortality.

Apart from family and close friends who were marvellous, neighbours rallied round and showed their concern for us. Meals were cooked and brought to the house; thoughtful people provided tea and coffee and even brought extra coffee mugs round to cope with all the visitors. Attention to such practical details was greatly appreciated as I was not capable of thinking logically. Several people sent me lovely bouquets of flowers for the home, as one person put it: "Just to show our love for you!"

People ask me if I was angry with God and I can truthfully say I wasn't. I was bewildered but not angry. In fact throughout this whole difficult time I felt the Lord was very close to me. It was as though He was saying: "I can't take your pain away - that's the price you pay when you love somebody - but I will be with you and I'll help you bear the pain."

The funeral directors asked me to choose clothes for Warren and it was a strange experience trying to pick an outfit for him in the circumstances. Although he'd converted to Catholicism, Warren remained a loyal Rangers fan. There was much good natured teasing went on in our house about this and if Celtic beat Rangers for instance, Warren would say: "Now Margaret, lay off those Hail Marys and give Rangers a break!" As I chose clothes to send to the funeral home, I had to smile as I included Warren's favourite Rangers tie; I was sure he would have approved.

The day of the funeral dawned bright and sunny. It was a beautiful May morning and I woke up very early and walked through the quiet house as though somehow I'd find Warren amongst all the familiar objects. I sat on the new sofa he had so recently chosen and reflected on how little time he'd had to enjoy it. Everything seemed empty and meaningless and Jesus' words came to mind:

"Do not store up treasures for yourselves on earth where moths and woodworms destroy them and thieves can break in and steal them. But store up treasures for yourselves in heaven where neither moths nor woodworms destroy them and thieves cannot break in and steal. For where your treasure is, there will your heart be also." (Matthew 6:19-21).

I had no doubt where Warren's heart lay and once more felt deeply grateful that God had given him the gift of faith.

Soon it would be time to get ready for the funeral and as the time drew I shuddered when I contemplated the day ahead. The thought of having to sit in the church alongside the coffin overwhelmed me. I had attended too many funerals:

it seemed my life had been full of bereavements and this was one too many. "God, you've got to help me. I can't go through with this". I was on my knees in the bathroom. "Strength will come when you need it." The words rose up in the silence of my heart.

I dressed carefully that morning, adding a generous spray of the perfume Warren had bought me at Christmas. By the time the funeral cars arrived I was composed and nobody would have guessed the turmoil I had experienced earlier. My sister told me later she'd felt sure I was not going to make it.

I had chosen the hymns for the requiem Mass very carefully. Warren always enjoyed lively upbeat music and was not shy in letting Jane, the organist, know what he thought of her choice of music on Sunday mornings. He would turn around and give her the 'thumbs up' if he enjoyed them or the 'thumbs down' if he thought they were 'dirges' as he called them. It was done with a good natured grin, and Jane took it in good part. I was determined there would be no dreary hymns, at his funeral!

The Mass was very comforting, emphasising that death is not the end for those who believe in Christ but the beginning of a new life with Him. Many people remarked later that they had gone into the church feeling sad but came out feeling uplifted, thanks to the joyful atmosphere of the service. Even those who were not regular church-goers remarked later how much they had enjoyed the service. One friend remarked: "It wasn't a bit morbid; I'm sure Warren would have given it the thumbs up!"

As we made our way to the cemetery set on a hill overlooking the city, it was like a dream sequence. I felt a sense of unreality as though I were watching events from a distance. The sun had been shining all morning but just as the coffin was lowered into the ground, a sudden shower of rain fell softly on the crowd. At the same time a friend nudged me and I looked on in amazement as a beautiful butterfly emerged from the grave. Butterflies are very significant for me and my house is full of pictures, plaques and various knick-knacks depicting butterflies. I even have some set into the windows in my conservatory.

As we sang the final hymn, "Amazing Grace," I gave thanks once more for the grace which had saved both Warren and myself from the destructive power of alcoholism. Many of those at the graveside were also recovering alcoholics and so it was appropriate that as Warren's body was finally laid to rest, we closed the ceremony with the prayer known as 'The Serenity Prayer' with which we close our AA meetings:

> *"God grant me the Serenity*
> *To accept the things I cannot change,*
> *Courage to change the things I can;*
> *And the wisdom to know the difference."*

This simple prayer sums up perfectly our needs. I cannot afford to live a life dominated with 'what ifs?' Verses 16-17 in Psalm 139 say that 'all of our days are recorded in your book before they have even begun' and this assures us that God does not have unexpected visitors! He knows exactly when each one of us will die. Just as we were leaving the cemetery the sun came out once more, reflecting upon drops of rain caught in the grass and a glorious rainbow arched across the sky, the ancient sign of God's promise of peace.

St. Paul in his letter to the Thessalonians says we are not to mourn, "like those who have no hope" (1.Thess.4:13); but he doesn't say do not mourn, and only those who have experienced the death of a loved one and the brutally sudden end of a loving relationship can really understand the intense pain involved. Many people seem unwilling or unable to handle another's grief and adopt a brisk air of false jollity, often refusing to speak about the dead person, as though they never existed! When I remarked recently upon the sudden death of a young man the glib reply came; "The Lord must have wanted him." These words are trite and not at all comforting for somebody who has just lost a loved one. The person who said this had never experienced the loss of anybody close, except the death of his parents who both lived well into their eighties.

People don't mean to be unkind but it is very hurtful when you see somebody deliberately cross the street rather than face you. Friends may feel at a loss for words when visiting the recently bereaved but often the best thing one can do is simply let the person cry. Bereaved people are not looking for words of wisdom and a simple gesture such as a touch of the hand is more comforting than empty words. The old saying "time is a great healer" is true but we must allow time to do its work. There is a season for all things; there is a time to rejoice and a time to mourn. Grief is a journey which can't be rushed.

Without my faith in God I'm sure I couldn't have coped

with this devastating loss and I truly experienced the reality of God's love at this difficult time. My faith didn't take away the pain because I believe there are no shortcuts through grief and it's a process which has various stages such as denial and anger which one has to experience before we reach a place of acceptance and peace. I felt as though I'd completely lost my bearings when Warren died and for a long time I could not even contemplate a future without him. One well meaning person said, "Now cheer up. Remember, Warren's with Jesus." I resisted the urge to say, "Would you like your husband to be with Jesus today?" Yes, I did believe Warren was with Jesus, but to be honest, at that moment I'd rather he was with me! Although we want our loved ones to go to heaven, we don't usually want them to go today!

CHAPTER FIFTEEN

Candles in the Dark

You have noted my agitation;
now collect my tears
in your wineskin.
(Psalms 56: 7)

After the funeral there were lots of practical matters to deal with and I realise now that I probably tried to do too much too soon. For instance, one morning less than a week after the funeral I had an appointment with the solicitor. During my drive into the city in the midst of heavy traffic, I heard a song on the radio which triggered a memory of Warren and I broke down and wept I could only turn the car around and go back home. Because I was due to go into hospital in just ten days time I was under pressure to get things in order and there were many important papers to sign.

For some months I had been experiencing health problems

and the specialist recommended that I have a hysterectomy. This was arranged months before Warren died and most people assumed I would cancel the operation in the circumstances. However I prayed about it and then discussed it with the specialist who asked me if I wanted to wait until I was feeling better emotionally. But as my daughter Sara said: "There's never going to be a 'good time' to have the operation in the near future Mum. If you postpone the surgery now you might never be able to face it." So I decided to go ahead and have the operation and it proved to be the right decision.

Although I have always felt ambivalent about private health care, I knew that I could not have coped in a large public ward full of strangers for my post operative recovery; my grief was just too raw. Because the surgery had been arranged before Warren died, I was covered by his company health scheme so I was able to have it done in a private hospital where at least I had the privacy of my own room.

"You mustn't drive for at least six weeks," the surgeon said. This was frustrating but I had to be sensible if I wanted to make a good recovery from what is after all major surgery. Fortunately friends rallied round to help with shopping until I could drive again and my sister Sheila came up from Barrow to look after the boys and I for the first few weeks. I really missed Warren's support at that time and I know he would have pampered me. No doubt if he had been there I would have been tempted to play the invalid for a little longer. As it was, I couldn't wait to get fit as soon as possible.

"You have made a remarkable recovery, especially in the circumstances," the doctor said at my post operative check-up. "What's your secret?" he joked. I told him about my faith in God and how so many people had been praying for me. "Well, I'm sure that was a factor" he said.

God often provides for our needs through the love of others and I certainly felt he provided through the tender loving care of my friends, Michael and Tessa McBrien. They are dear friends who invited me and the boys to stay with them shortly after my operation. I felt we needed a break but I couldn't face taking the boys off on holiday alone, so we gratefully accepted their offer to spend some time at their beautiful home in Suffolk. The three of us were in need of tender loving care and certainly received it at the hands of these dear people. Tessa is a wonderful cook whose chocolate brownies are legendary and Michael, who was at that time an eminent surgeon working in the local hospital, was on hand to take care of any medical problems.

One day Tessa took the boys and me to London where we visited the newly refurbished Jewel House in the Tower. We were fortunate to see the Crown Jewels that afternoon as later that evening a tremendous storm broke over London and the heavens opened, flooding the Jewel House. Looking at those priceless gems, it struck me that what I have today, since I found the Lord, is far more precious than anything in those closely guarded display cases. I realised that I have found the 'pearl of great price' that Jesus talked about (Matt 13:44) and my relationship with Him is the most important thing in my life. Later, as I watched the boys enjoying the exhibits at the Natural History Museum

in Kensington, their sorrow forgotten for a moment, I
thanked God for taking such good care of us and blessing us
through the love of friends. He really does provide for all of
our needs.

Some people said: "How come if God is so good, He took
your husband?" One person even went so far as to say: "We
thought God really loved you!" - the implication being that
in fact He didn't! But Warren and I were not afraid of death,
believing that our life span is in God's hands and that we
will not die before our time. As it happens, Warren was in
the habit of reading the "Daily Light" devotional book
every morning, and by a remarkable 'coincidence' on April
27th, the day he died, the reading was very appropriate:
"My brothers, there is not much time left. The world and
everything in it that people desire is passing away; but
he who does the will of God lives forever... Death is
destroyed, victory is complete."

Warren could not have known how uncannily prophetic
those words would prove to be for him before the end of the
day. I take comfort from knowing that our lives are in God's
hands and that what happened to Warren was within His
divine providence.

Warren and I had planned to take the boys to the New
Dawn Conference at Walsingham that year and I decided
to go ahead as planned. It was both a very blessed time
and a very painful experience for me. The boys refused to
take part in any of the children's activities, preferring
instead to wander around rather aimlessly until that is they
discovered the Holy Spirit Chapel. If ever I wanted to find

them I could be sure to find them in there, gazing at the dozens of candles reflected in the mosaics on the walls. For some reason they were fascinated by this special little chapel and it was as though the Lord himself was putting His arms around these two lonely little boys and comforting them.

There is a prie dieu in the chapel with a beautiful prayer on it. It is the prayer of the late Cardinal Mercier and has become very precious to me:

> *O, Holy Spirit, beloved of my soul,*
> *I adore you,*
> *Enlighten, guide,*
> *Strengthen and console me.*
> *Tell me what I should do*
> *And command me to do it.*
> *I promise to submit myself*
> *To all that you desire of me*
> *And to accept all*
> *That you permit*
> *To happen to me.*
> *Let me only know your will.*

Although it is a huge struggle at times, I know that if I am willing to surrender daily to God's will, my life is in safe hands.

At the New Dawn Conference that year I felt Warren's absence keenly and it was difficult to concentrate on the talks. I began to think I'd made a terrible mistake in coming so soon after his death. However, an incident occurred one day that convinced me that I was in fact in the right place.

As I was walking across the fields between the marquees, I was stopped in my tracks by Father Bob Faricy, a well known Jesuit priest and one of the speakers. Lost in my own thoughts, I was startled when he said: "Excuse me ma'am but the Lord just told me to tell you not to worry about your husband. He's in heaven right now!" He looked as surprised as I was and taking me to one side, he asked me when my husband had died. I was astonished; here was somebody who'd never set eyes on me before, knew nothing about me and yet the Lord had given him powerful words of comfort for me.

Actually, the day before, I'd attended a talk given by Father Faricy, as there was a large group of us it was decided that rather than sit in a stuffy tent, we should sit out on the grass. As I sat in the warm afternoon sun I was only half listening to the talk as my spirit was so heavy. Suddenly Father Bob stopped in mid sentence and said that he was getting words of scripture coming to his mind which he felt were for somebody in the crowd. He said: "I don't usually do this; this is Sr. Lucy's gift," referring to Sr. Lucy Rooney who often ministered with Fr. Bob. He went on to quote Baruch 5:1-4 saying: "This is for somebody here, and the Lord will confirm it." My friend who was sitting next to me dug me in the ribs and whispered that's for you! She said this because only that morning she had bought me a little prayer card bearing this particular verse of scripture which seemed apt for my situation. I was deeply touched and humbled that the Lord should be so gracious as to comfort me in this way. These two incidents gave me enormous courage to carry on in the knowledge that God was firmly in charge and that I could trust Him to take care of our little family.

Several days later I was in the abbey ruins waiting for Mass to start when Babsie Bleasdale walked by. At that time Babsie had an international ministry and was a well known speaker. My friend Helen who had known Babsie for many years grabbed her arm and introduced her to me. Babsie put her big strong arms around me and hugged me. When you've been hugged by Babsie you really know all about it! She's a wonderful Trinidadian lady whom the Lord uses powerfully in ministering His love and truths to people throughout the world. After my friend told Babsie what had happened to Warren and that my first husband had died too, Babsie hugged me and whispered: "God is a jealous God. I think He wants you for Himself now." Although I knew Babsie was trying to comfort me, I didn't want to hear these words. What did it mean? That I was to spend the rest of my life alone? I felt like saying: "Please Lord, would you mind finding somebody else?" I smiled politely and thanked Babsie but hoped that she was wrong!

I had many dreams in the weeks and months following Warren's death when my subconscious fears were revealed. In one dream, I was in a small boat with Warren, Michael and Tony. We were out in the middle of a calm sea when suddenly a fierce storm blew up and threw us all into the sea. Somehow the boys and I managed to scramble back into the boat but Warren was nowhere to be seen. A terrible sense of panic overwhelmed me as I realised that Warren had the maps and navigating equipment and now they were lost and we were all alone in a vast ocean. When I woke up, I felt a deep sadness and anxiety until a still small voice within said: "Don't worry, I am the Way." I realised that the One who had just spoken in my spirit was He who is The Way, The Truth, and The Life.

Another time I dreamt that I was following Warren along a narrow high sided canyon when we reached a dead end and Warren suddenly disappeared. I was all alone in this frightening place and then I turned around and saw that the path was in fact filled with light and quickly found my way to safety. I interpreted this dream as revealing my fear of spending my future alone and the Lord's reassurance that in fact I would never be alone as He is always with me. There are times when I may feel lonely but in fact I am never alone.

Like all widows I have had to learn new skills. I am glad that electrical goods are fitted with plugs these days, although I can rewire a plug when necessary now! That first summer without Warren was a painful and difficult time when even a visit to the local supermarket reminded me of my loss. Whilst choosing some flowers for Warren's grave one day, I overheard two women discussing their plans for the evening.

"I mustn't forget the spare ribs!" one of them said. "John just loves barbecues. You'd think he was the world's greatest chef when he's behind that grill; but ask him to cook anything in the kitchen? No chance!"

"I know" her friend laughed. "George is exactly the same! Men!" she said with mock exasperation. Whilst they were busy planning to spend a pleasant evening with their husbands, I was going to put flowers on my dear husband's grave. I hurriedly paid for the flowers and left. When I got to the car I broke down and wept. What would become of me and how could I possibly face the future alone?

CHAPTER SIXTEEN

In the Shadow of His Wings

Father of orphans, defender of widows;
such is God in His holy dwelling.
God gives the lonely a permanent home
(Psalms 68: 5-6)

There are many painful situations to deal with in the first year of widowhood, for instance all the special occasions that have to be faced alone such as birthdays, anniversaries, and Christmas. That first Christmas I had to make a supreme effort for the sake of the boys to try to resume normal life. In actual fact I could have earned an Oscar for my performance! Whilst my heart was breaking, I tried to appear cheerful and optimistic and people commented on how well I was doing. If only they'd known the heartache which I hid with a smile and the numbers of tears I shed once I had closed my bedroom door at night.

But you soon realise that in the midst of your sorrow, life goes on for everybody else and you just cannot burden people. The only place I could go was to the Lord and although I still felt intense sorrow, I knew that He was close by and that He cared deeply for the boys and I. God seems to have a soft spot for 'widows and orphans' judging by the number of references to them in scripture and I found this immensely comforting. It was not 'pie in the sky when you die' but a deeply felt reality.

A year after Warren's death, I decided to take the boys on holiday to Ibiza and Sara agreed to come with us. I was glad of her help as I couldn't have coped alone. Although I tried to enjoy myself for their sake, my heart was not really in it and seeing all the happy families sitting together in the hotel dining room or having fun on the beach only intensified my sense of loss. I was painfully reminded that no matter where I go in the world Warren will never be there and when I come back home, he will not be there either.

By the time Sunday came, after having spent a lot of time on the crowded beach which just compounded my sense of loneliness, I was in need of Christian fellowship but the thought of attending Mass in a foreign language amongst strangers didn't appeal to me. After making enquiries at the hotel I discovered there is an English church in Ibiza but as it was on the other side of the island I would have to hire a car as there was no public transport. Like many women I had always let my husband do the driving when we were abroad and the thought of hiring a car and driving on the right hand side of the road along the winding coastal route was daunting. However, taking my courage in both hands and whispering a quick prayer I set off. Sara took the boys on a boat trip, so I was quite alone. The first few miles were nerve-wracking but the opening lines of Psalm 91 came to mind: "He who dwells in the shadow of the almighty need fear no harm." I eventually reached the little church in one piece and walked in just in time to hear the congregation reciting those very words! God's timing is incredible.

I thoroughly enjoyed the lively service which lifted my spirits and afterwards I joined the regulars for coffee in the local café. Coffee stretched into lunch and afternoon tea and the sun was setting by the time I got back to the hotel. It had been a blessed day and I felt sure that Warren would have approved of my excursion. He was a great encourager who frequently challenged me to step out and have a bit more confidence in myself and I knew he would urge me to put my trust in God and not be afraid of what the future might hold. I have found that God can be trusted to take care of us, if only we will truly surrender our lives to Him, which is easier said than done, as most of us want to be in control of our own lives.

Once on my way to visit a friend in Australia, I spent a few days in Hong Kong and as the plane prepared for landing, I began to feel a little anxious. Travelling alone is not easy and I don't relish arriving in a strange country where there is nobody to meet me or help me find my way around. As my anxiety grew, I shot up a quick prayer: "Lord, you'll have to help me. I don't speak the language and I don't know where I'm going. Please help me to get to the hotel safely." Moments later, the young man in the seat next to me, who'd been asleep for most of the flight, struck up a conversation. He told me that he was on a business trip and after exchanging a few pleasantries he turned to look out of the window. Suddenly without any preamble he turned around: "By the way, where are you staying while you're in Hong Kong?" When I told him the name of the hotel, he smiled and said: "Oh, that's where I always stay. In fact my company will be sending a limousine to pick me up. Can I offer you a lift?" This young man whose name was Darren was truly an answer to prayer as he not only took me to the hotel in a large air conditioned limousine, but he also carried my bags!

Later that evening Darren joined me for dinner. He turned to me at one point saying, "'I don't know what on earth made me offer you a lift like that. I'm not in the habit of inviting strange ladies into the company car!" He laughed when I confessed that I'd just said a wee prayer moments before he offered to help me. "Well, it certainly worked!"

St. James tells us:" You do not have, because you do not ask God" (James 4:2). I believe the more we ask of God, the more opportunities we give Him to demonstrate His unfailing love and concern for us and there have been many instances during my travels when help has been forthcoming as a direct answer to prayer.

It is estimated that it takes at least two years to come to terms with the death of a loved one and I would agree. I seemed to be making headway when grief would suddenly catch me unawares. I liken it to being on a beach at low tide when suddenly without warning a huge wave sweeps in and knocks you off your feet.

Once when I was walking through a shopping mall I heard a piece of music which reminded me of Warren and I promptly burst into tears to the surprise of the startled shoppers. Again the Lord provided for me in my time of need as a fellow parishioner 'just happened' to walk through the busy mall at that very moment and helped me back to the car where we sat and talked for a while. Incidents such as this were embarrassing at times but I just had to take each day as it came. Having the boys to take care of helped me not to dwell too much on my own pain.

"Will you always be like this Mum?" asked Michael anxiously as he came in from school one day and found me in tears yet again. I tried not to let the boys see me crying too often because I didn't want them to worry about me. They had their own sorrow to cope with. Looking at Michael's worried little face, I tried to reassure him. "No, Mike. It won't always be like this. Nobody could feel this bad forever."

Michael had started secondary school shortly after Warren's death and that first year was difficult. I was often called to the school to discuss his behaviour, which was at times disruptive. Eventually it was agreed that an educational psychologist might be able to help him. After meeting several times with Michael, the psychologist came to the house to discuss his findings with me.

"Don't worry too much about Michael. He's not a bad boy." he said, "It's just his way of coping with his father's death. Attention seeking is just part of how Michael is dealing with his grief. Children can't verbalise their feelings in the way that adults can and sometimes disruptive behaviour is their way of expressing their feelings. He is angry about his father's death and he feels helpless. But he has a supportive family and I'm sure he will come through this in time." Thankfully, things settled down at school and Michael has grown up to be a fine young man, but on reflection I wonder if I was so wrapped up in my own grief that I wasn't able to help the boys deal appropriately with theirs.

Tony is a different personality, keeping his feelings to himself. One day however when he couldn't find his Game Boy, he broke down and wept bitterly. He was inconsolable and a friend who was staying with us at the time wisely pointed out that it was probably not the loss of the gadget he was really crying about, but the loss of his Dad. As I felt the boys needed me to be at home at this time, I was not in a hurry to go back to work but I needed something apart from housework to occupy my mind.

"Have you ever thought of studying for a degree, Margaret?" Sister Josephine had once asked me. "Me, get a degree?" I laughed. "You must be joking. I'm too old for one thing; besides, I don't think I've got the brains and it's over thirty years since I left school! How could I possibly go to university at my age?"

The idea seemed preposterous; like many women I had very little confidence in my abilities after being away from full time education for so long. Nevertheless, the seed had been planted and after meeting a woman of my own age who was studying for a degree at Aberdeen University, I began to consider the idea. Shortly afterwards, I read an article in the local press about something called the Access Course; a special course designed to give mature students entry to university. As the university was practically on my doorstep, I decided to make some enquiries. In due course I attended an interview and discovered there was a variety of interesting foundation courses on offer.

"Well, I've got nothing to lose; I suppose I could give it a try?" After completing the necessary paperwork I was accepted and in September 1996, with much trepidation, I began the one year Access Course at Aberdeen University.

CHAPTER SEVENTEEN

The Years the Locusts Ate

The fear of the Lord is the beginning of Wisdom
(Proverbs 9: 10)
(Aberdeen University Motto)

Despite my initial fears and chronic anxiety, I took to the academic life immediately and with great enthusiasm applied myself to my studies. After successfully completing the Access Course, I was accepted as an undergraduate and began studying for an MA Honours Degree in English Literature. I decided that if I was going to study, it might as well be something I enjoyed and as I have always loved reading, English was the logical choice. When people asked why I didn't study theology I jokingly replied: "Because I don't want to lose my faith!" There's more than a grain of truth in that actually as I've seen the results of studying scripture as just one more academic subject. Whilst I'm not decrying the serious study of scripture, and in fact am currently studying theology, there is a danger that scholars can intellectualise the Word of God to such an extent that its life-changing power is neutralised. If we have mere 'head knowledge' with no experience of the Holy Spirit, scripture study can be reduced to just one more academic subject.

I have attended lectures at university when the lecturer was keen to 'de-mythologise' the scriptures. Determined to explain away the miracles of Jesus, he was keen to offer 'rational and logical explanations' more appropriate to these 'enlightened' times. At the risk of being called naïve, I am quite happy to believe that Jesus walked on water and actually fed a crowd of thousands with a few loaves and fishes. Somebody once said: "God said it, I believe it, and that settles it!" - a sentiment with which I totally agree.

Initially my time at university was a bit daunting, sitting in lectures with young people who were fresh out of school, and I wondered how the students in my tutorial groups would feel about having a grandmother in their midst. However, I found them to be open and friendly and they even invited me to join them in the pub after classes. However, unlike them, I had responsibilities at home and two boys to take care of, but it was nice to feel accepted.

I can't pretend it was easy being a full time student as well as a Mum to two teenage boys who needed a lot of attention and it required time management skills. The MA degree takes four years in Scotland and Scottish Universities have a broad approach to an MA; instead of focusing on just one subject you are expected to take three subjects in first year, two in second year and by the third year students decide whether they will study for a joint or single Honours degree for their final two years. Although I enjoyed studying Sociology, I finally decided that as my great love was English literature, I should concentrate on that and do single Honours.

At times it was difficult trying to find time to spend in the library and meet the deadlines for essays on top of all my other responsibilities but somehow I managed and even gained good marks for my essays. One definite advantage I had over the young students was the fact that I had already sowed my wild oats, and unlike many of them, I didn't go partying and was not hung-over at weekends! The university library is usually a pretty quiet place on Saturday and Sunday mornings!

During the summer in the year before graduation I decided to take the plunge and do some voluntary work in America. Many students spend their summers working in children's camps in the States and whilst I didn't particularly fancy doing that, it gave me the idea that perhaps there was something useful I could do which would combine some holiday time too.

After checking out various Catholic volunteer sites on the internet, I contacted the Sisters of St. Joseph in Boston who run a volunteer programme each summer. They were keen to welcome me as their first oversees volunteer and their oldest to date! And so in the summer of 2000, I found myself enjoying the warmth of a New England summer.

Boston is a lovely city and as it is relatively old by American standards, it was built with pedestrians and horse-drawn vehicles in mind and unlike most American cities is quite easy to navigate on foot. During my free time I enjoyed walking the Freedom Trail and visiting the ship where they re-enact the famous 'Boston Tea Party' for visitors. There are splendid museums and art galleries and the ever popular Boston Common was crowded with visitors simply enjoying a seat in the sun, watching the world go by. There was plenty to occupy me during my free time.

I had a comfortable room at Mount St. Joseph and enjoyed the company of the sisters and my fellow volunteers immensely. It was decided that as I was studying English, I should teach English as a second language and although I had no experience in this, the Sister in charge was very encouraging and said I was 'a natural' and before long I was teaching a variety of immigrants from all parts of the world.

It was challenging at times trying to teach people who had varying needs and who came from a variety of back-grounds. Amongst my students there was Carla, an Italian doctor who wanted to improve her grammar; Anya, a widowed psychiatrist from Kiev who had come to live with her daughter in Boston; Angelica, a housewife from Guatemala who wanted to be able to converse with her children in English and Han, a computer expert from China. They were a delightful group and it taxed my ingenuity to devise classes which would be interesting for all of them. I thoroughly enjoyed the teaching and actually gained valuable skills in this area.

After an enjoyable summer in Boston, I said goodbye to

my new friends and headed home. Whilst checking in for my flight at Boston's Logan Airport, I had an interesting experience. I had arrived early to check in my bags and was the first person at the desk. As I looked at the rather formidable looking lady who was checking in my luggage, I received what is often referred to as 'a word of knowledge' about her. The first time this had happened to me was whilst I was praying with others in a prayer ministry team and the leader asked if anybody had any 'words' or impressions about the person we were praying for. I became aware of a 'picture' forming in my mind which turned out to be very accurate and appropriate for the person and enabled the group to pray powerfully into the situation. The group leader explained afterwards that God gives these words of knowledge to help us minister to others and is a gift or charism of the Holy Spirit.

As I stood at the check in desk, I felt the Lord say: "This woman is a Catholic but she hasn't been to Mass for a long time. I want you to tell her how much I love her." My immediate reaction was: "You must be joking Lord! Please tell her yourself!" As I stood there, I became more and more uncomfortable. How do you say such a thing to a complete stranger and what if I was just imagining it? She might think I was a madwoman and send for the security guards? But the thought persisted and so plucking up courage I said "I think you're a Catholic aren't you? But you haven't been to Mass lately?"

The startled woman looked up as she was putting a tag on my suitcase and said, "How do you know that?" Feeling rather foolish I said: "I know this must sound strange, but I

feel the Lord just told me that and he also said to tell you
that he loves you very much." As I spoke, tears filled her
eyes and she said bitterly: "No, I don't go to church now,
there's no point. The church doesn't want me!" As the
queue was building up behind me I didn't have time to ask
her what she meant by that but guessed that at some time
she'd been hurt by somebody in a position of authority in
the church. As I picked up my boarding pass, I said "Don't
turn your back on the Lord even if you feel the church has
let you down. Please remember Jesus loves you very
much." As I walked off she said softly, "Thank you ma'am.
You don't know how much that means to me." I don't
know what the outcome of that encounter was but I'd done
my part. It was between her and the Lord now.

Once when I said to the Lord: "Lord, what's the point of the
talks I do and all the times I've told people about you. I
never see any results; am I just wasting my time?" I felt a
gentle voice within say: "Mind your own business. You
don't have to see results Margaret. Just scatter the seed as I
give it to you. Be faithful and leave the results to me. It is
my harvest, not yours." The Lord has a wonderfully gentle
way of rebuking us at times without condemning us. So
that put me in my place! From then on I no longer worried
about the outcome of my encounters with others. All I have
to do is be obedient; the results are in God's hands.

I returned to university refreshed after my summer break.
It had been a time of learning for me as well as a holiday. I
had one more year of disciplined study and research ahead
of me and I determined to give it my best shot. After much
hard work I finally handed in my dissertation in May 2001

and in June was delighted to learn that I had been awarded an Upper Second Class Honours Degree, which wasn't bad for somebody who had been out of full time education for over thirty years; and who I had thought was 'too stupid' to go to university.

It was a very emotional day for me when my children joined me for the degree ceremony and I was reminded of the words of scripture where God promises to restore the years the locusts ate. The locusts in my life were anger and self-destruction, fuelled by alcohol, but my convent education had stood me in good stead and God had given me a second chance to make up for the time I had wasted in my youth.

By now the boys were grown up and working for local oil companies. I felt that I had been blessed in many ways and wanted to make some useful contribution to society if possible so I checked out various volunteer sites on the internet as I'd enjoyed my stint the previous summer in Boston. I contacted several religious communities in the States who offered volunteer placements and was invited to join a Benedictine community in Kansas for a year.

It's not easy trying to set your house in order for a whole year and after a hectic couple of weeks sorting things out so that the boys could run the house as smoothly as possible whilst I was away, I was ready to go. Friends wondered how I dared leave two young men in charge of a house and the cats for so long, but I knew my boys could handle it. Since their father had died, they'd had to grow up pretty fast and I had wanted them to be as independent as possible and certainly hadn't pampered them! They were both quite accomplished cooks by now and capable of taking care of themselves. Also if I truly believed that God was in charge I just had to trust Him to take care of them – and my house!

After an uneventful flight I arrived in Dallas where I was to get a connecting flight to Kansas City. As it was my entry point into the States I had to go through US Customs and Immigration before I boarded my onward flight. I was confident that all my papers were in order, having obtained a one year volunteer's visa through the US Embassy in London and had no reason to expect any difficulties. However, as it turned out I suffered an unpleasant interrogation by an Immigration Officer whose attitude was openly hostile. For some reason she couldn't seem to grasp why anybody would leave their home to work in a foreign country for free!

"Don't you have a home?" she demanded. "Don't you have qualifications? Do you realise I have the power to send you straight home on the next flight?" She almost hissed at me. I couldn't understand her aggressiveness but thankfully I remained calm and simply said: "Yes, I'm sure you do. But why would you want to do that?" After a tense interview, during which I was made to feel like a homeless bag lady, the officer finally slammed her stamp on my passport saying: "You can stay for six months only!"

I was puzzled: I had prayed long and hard about this place-ment and I couldn't understand why things seemed to be going wrong before I even got there. In all my visits to the United States I'd never met such rudeness and hostility from Immigration Officials. Ironically this was the day before the terrible events of 11th September, 2001. I could have more readily understood her attitude if I had been travelling in the immediate aftermath of the terrorist attacks but I could think of no explanation for her aggressive behaviour. However, as I boarded the onward flight to Kansas City I felt a sense of peace despite the unpleasant experience I'd just had, and I sensed that God was in charge of the whole situation. Although I was puzzled by the experience, I knew I could trust the Lord.

I went to the monastery hoping to teach English on a special programme for High School dropouts and also to do voluntary work with alcoholics in a rehab centre, but it didn't work out as planned and instead I was asked to work in the laundry, the bakery and the retreat centre where I was put to work as a cleaner. I had nothing against domestic work; it's just that I had hoped to be able to use my new-found skills and perhaps had something to offer those in rehab, having been myself set free from addiction to alcohol.

"Lord, did I come six thousand miles just to clean toilets? I can do that at home!" I felt the Lord say: "My child, you thought you came out here to do, but I want to teach you how to just be."

I didn't understand at first but as the months went by I realised that God was teaching me a valuable lesson. I realised that I still felt I had to achieve things for God in order to please Him, as though I had to prove my worth to Him.

We live in a society which values quantifiable results and this can spill over into our spiritual life too, as though the busier we are the more important we must be to God. In fact we don't have to prove anything to Him and sometimes the more we toil the less we seem to achieve.

Scripture tells us that: "Unless the Lord builds the house, the labourers toil in vain" (Psalm 127:1). So although I still didn't really see the point of travelling thousands of miles to do domestic work, I determined to do my best, no matter how humble and mundane the tasks I was given and stopped worrying about whether or not I was 'achieving' anything for the Lord. My time in Kansas proved to be a steep learning curve for me. I discovered how God's plans often differ from mine and sometimes what I think is a good idea is not always a God idea!

The sisters were disappointed when I told them I could only stay for six months instead of a year and contacted the Immigration Department on my behalf. The officials there assured me they would be happy to grant an extension so that I could stay until August as planned. However, I had a strong sense that I should just stay for six months after all. I had learned to follow that inner leading and although I didn't understand why, I felt sure it was God's plan that I return home in February.

As part of my duties in the monastery, I had to spend several hours a day at a reception desk where I was supposed to direct visitors to the administration centre. At first I found it rather tedious until I began to take a notebook along with me and discovered a hidden talent for writing poetry, some of which was published in the Kansas State poetry magazine. Also, this building was linked to the sisters' accommodation and many of the elderly sisters particularly loved to stop and chat with me. I'd often share stories of the Lord's goodness with them and one of them christened my desk 'The Wayside Pulpit.' "Do you realise you're evangelising us?" one elderly nun said one day. "Maybe we were getting kind of stale and we needed a shakeup!" she chuckled.

The sisters had been gifted a small house situated on a beautiful nearby lake which they used for rest and recreation. One cold but beautiful day in January I went out there to spend some time alone. My time in the convent was drawing to a close and I felt the need to go off and pray about my future.

Although it was mid-winter and the migrating snow geese should have been further south by then; because there was a channel of warm water from a nearby power station which fed into the lake, the water was not frozen and there was still plenty of food for the birds. I stood at the lakeside and watched the geese. There were hundreds of beautiful white snow geese gathered on the surface and it was a breathtaking sight. Snow lay all around and the air was crystal clear and perfectly still.

Suddenly the silence was broken as the huge flock rose into the air in what was almost a single movement. I wondered what had startled them and then I saw it. A large eagle was circling around swooping lower and lower until finally he swooped down onto the surface of the lake and snatched one of the beautiful geese. I was joined by a man walking his dog and we watched for a moment in silence as the eagle carried off his prey. We both agreed that nature can be cruel at times. "You see, that old eagle's been biding his time," he said. "He was looking for a weak one. Once he found him, all he had to do was spook the whole flock into flying then grab that sick one that was left behind!"

Later that day I reflected on what I'd witnessed on the lake, comparing it to the Christian life. Just like that sick goose we need community and the support of others who journey with us. If we're isolated we become an easy target for the devil. I suddenly felt vulnerable as I realised what a spiritual battle we are in. I was conscious of just how little I really knew about the bible. The thought persisted that I really needed to learn more about the Word of God and I prayed that I might find some way of being able to study and deepen my understanding of it.

My time in Kansas was almost at an end and on the day before I was due to leave for home I attended a poetry reading group. Afterwards a few of us went to a local restaurant where I had a long chat with one of the writers. People often tell me their life stories for some reason and Gloria was no exception! She confided that she was an adopted child and had always wondered how her mother could have given her up. She was very bitter in fact and obviously held a grudge against her natural mother, whom she'd never met.

I listened quietly while she vented her anger and then shared a little of my story with her. I told her of the circumstances which had led to my having given my much loved baby up for adoption. As I spoke, Gloria broke down and wept, oblivious to the stares we were attracting. After she'd composed herself, she took my hand saying: "Honey, this was no coincidence that I met you today. It was a God incidence!" Gloria has since told me that meeting me and hearing my side of the story helped her forgive her mother and accept that she probably hadn't wanted to part with her baby any more than I had.

"It was a real healing experience, Margaret. And I can't believe I just met you the day before you were leaving the States. God sure cuts it kinda fine at times!" Since then I have been back to Kansas on holiday, staying at the home of Gloria and her dear husband John. They are larger than life characters and their home reflects this! I was somewhat surprised when I walked into their living room to see a gleaming vintage Harley Davidson motorcycle had pride of place in the centre of the room. And as a finishing touch, a large fluffy chimpanzee sat proudly astride! Apparently the bike is so valuable they were afraid to leave it in the garage and as John doesn't use it now, it was in pristine condition. Outside the bathroom, a large cutout figure of John Wayne stands guard, whilst in the bedroom a similar sized model of Elvis Presley smiles benevolently! The house was filled with all kinds of knick knacks and reminded me of the 'The Old Curiosity Shop.'

Whilst sightseeing with Gloria and John, they took me to the neighbouring state of Missouri. We visited a tobacco farm where we saw the huge tobacco leaves hanging up to dry from the rafters of the barns. The workmen just happened to be having their lunch break and were happy to chat with a visitor from the UK and there was some good natured teasing about Sir Walter Raleigh and his discovery of tobacco! Much to my embarrassment, Gloria told them I was an evangelist and one of them promptly said, "Ok, ma'am, go ahead and preach!"

At first I think they were a little cynical as they leant back in their chairs and drew deeply on their cigarettes. Never one to refuse a challenge I plunged right in and shared a little of my life story. I told them that Jesus loves them too and I was touched to see tears in the eyes of these sun-scorched labourers amid much clearing of throats. "Why thank you Ma'am. That sure was fine!" One of the craggy labourers pumped my arm so hard I thought it would break. I felt humbled and privileged to have had the opportunity to share a little of the love of God in this unusual setting.

When it came time to leave the Benedictine sisters it was with genuine sadness. I had made many good friends in the community and had learned a lot about myself whilst I was there. The sisters had been very welcoming and had embraced me as part of their community. I had also made good friends at the local AA meetings I had attended each week. One of these new friends took me to the airport and as we parted company he said: "Remember Margaret, God has a plan for your life. This was just a small piece of the puzzle but he's got a whole lot more pieces out there before you see the whole picture!" I returned home at the beginning of February and as it turned out, I didn't have long to wait for the next piece of the puzzle to fall into place.

CHAPTER EIGHTEEN

Forgiveness Sets You Free

For the word of the Lord is living and active;
sharper than any double-edged sword
(Hebrews 11: 12)

"What do you plan to do now, Margaret?" asked my friend Helen. "Well, whilst I was in the States I realised that I am pretty ignorant about the scriptures and would really love an opportunity to study them but I wouldn't know where to start. There don't seem to be many opportunities for lay-people to study the bible."

"Well" she replied, "that's funny you should say that because I saw a course advertised in The Tablet that I'm sure would suit you perfectly." Helen quickly fetched the advertisement and as I read about the five month long Dei Verbum course I felt excited. The course, run by the Divine Word Missionaries (SVDs), offered scripture studies to both religious and laity and sounded ideal.

I posted off my application at once but as the months went by and I had still had no response, I was sure I'd been turned down. However, when I finally emailed Father Tim, the course director, he assured me that he had not received an application from me and said in any case it was too late now as all the places had been allocated for that year. I was disappointed as the course had seemed to be just what I was looking for and I was too impatient to wait until next year. Mindful that we are in a spiritual battle and determined not to give up at the first hurdle, I felt prompted to send off another application by email this time.

Just as I'd resigned myself to the fact that it wasn't going to happen, I received some surprising information from Rome. Father Tim had made enquiries locally and discovered that a postman had been stealing mail. At least that explained why they hadn't received my application. The postman probably thought the bulky envelope addressed to a missionary society contained money and when he found it didn't, he dumped it. I felt angry and disappointed to think that because of a stranger's dishonesty my plans had been thwarted. Good Christian that I am, I could cheerfully have strangled that postman if I'd got my hands on him! But as I was inwardly fuming and breathing dire threats against the unknown postman, I heard a quiet inner voice. "Will you forgive him?"

"Forgive him Lord, why should I? He spoiled my plans!" There was no reply. The answer was obvious; I must forgive because I had been forgiven for far worse things than stealing mail. As I struggled with my thoughts, the story of the unforgiving debtor came to mind. In Matthew's

Gospel, Jesus tells a story about a man who having had his own large debt cancelled by his employer, flew into a rage with his fellow servant who owed him a small sum of money, insisting that the poor man be thrown into prison (Matt 18:23-35).

By now, I felt suitably chastised and began to think about this man in Italy who had stolen mail. He must have been desperate to jeopardise his job and risk imprisonment and I wondered what had driven him to this point. Perhaps it wasn't just greed; maybe he had gambling debts or was into drugs? Only God knew the truth. But as I felt the Lord had asked me to forgive this man, how could I refuse? And so I knelt down there and then and began to pray for him.

"Lord, I do forgive him. And Lord, I also ask you to bless him and his family and bring him back onto the right path." I felt my disturbed feelings melt away and my anger was replaced by a sense of peace. The situation was out of my hands so I tried to let go of my disappointment and move on with my life.

The very next day I received an email from Rome informing me that the selection committee had decided it was unfair that I should be denied a place on the course because of somebody else's dishonesty. In the circumstances they agreed to make an exception and invited me to join the course at the end of August. I was overwhelmed when I thought of my initial reaction and how angry I'd been. It was by the grace of God that I'd been able to forgive the man who had stood in my way and in doing so I was in turn released from unforgiveness and bitterness which are so damaging.

It has been suggested that unforgiveness can cause much physical illness. Certainly I believe unforgiveness binds us and is like walking around with a ball and chain. As soon as I had forgiven, I was immediately released from my anger and resentment. It is not always easy to forgive, especially if we have been betrayed by friends or family, but I believe forgiveness is not about feelings but involves a decision. I may not feel like forgiving somebody who has really hurt me, but if I am at least willing to forgive them, God's grace will do the rest. Jesus tells us that we must forgive others before we ask God to forgive us and I felt I had learned a valuable lesson.

The Dei Verbum course started in late August and the next few weeks were hectic as I put things in order at home and tried to figure out just what to pack to cover five months in Italy. I was sure that it would be much warmer than Scotland and certainly I wouldn't need rainwear. Famous last words!

The day I arrived in Rome there was a fierce storm and tropical downpour and for the next few days Rome was more like Venice. The course was actually held in Nemi, a small town in the Albanian Hills close to the Pope's summer residence of Castel Gandolfo. Nemi is a medieval town perched on the edge of a volcanic lake, famed for its pizza restaurants and ice cream parlours; I knew I'd be very happy to spend the next five months there! However, as it is much higher above sea level than Rome, it is also much cooler and they had the coldest autumn and earliest winter they'd had in fifty years - so much for my hopes of escaping to the sun!

The Dei Verbum group was made up of twenty-nine students from all over the world. Out of this group, only five of us were lay people, the rest were priests and religious. In addition to our group, there were twenty-two missionary priests staying on campus who were attending a five month renewal course and as we shared mealtimes and recreation time, it made for a very lively community.

We were taught by a number of different lecturers, each specialising in a particular area of the Bible, covering various aspects of the Old and New Testaments. We learnt the basics of hermeneutics and exegesis and although five months is a not long in relation to studying the bible, we learned a lot in a short time.

The course was very intensive, running as it did for five days a week from nine in the morning until early evening. In addition to our weekly assignments, each student had to devise a suitable programme for scripture sharing in small groups as an end of course project. I entitled my project; Encountering Jesus in John's Gospel and I focused on Jesus' meetings with various individuals such as Nicodemus, the Samaritan woman and the man born blind. I contrasted their openness in response to meeting Jesus in comparison with the closed minds of the Pharisees and religious leaders of the day.

Apart from the actual course itself, living in community with such a diverse group of people from different cultures and backgrounds was a learning experience that was both challenging and enriching. I made many good friends during my time at Nemi, some of whom I have since visited at their mission stations around the world.

Another enjoyable aspect of the course was the opportunity we had of exploring Rome on our free days. I grew to love the city and apart from the breathtaking architecture and churches, discovered many other places of interest, including wonderful shops and restaurants!

The course finished shortly before Christmas and there was sadness as well as joy when we were presented with our diplomas by the Father General of the SVDs. It was hard saying goodbye as we knew that most of us would probably never meet again. However I would be seeing some of them soon, as one of the priests had invited me to spend the New Year with his family in Poland and several others had invited me to visit their mission stations in India.

I first became friendly with Father Andrzej who prefers to be known as Fr. Andrew, because we both enjoyed swimming and as the SVDs have a small beach house at Anzio, a group of us went there on Sundays to enjoy the quiet beach once the summer crowds had left. Father Andrew shared stories of his life as a missionary in Papua New Guinea where he had spent the previous twelve years and we discovered we had the same zany humour.

One day he asked me why I always seemed so happy and I shared a little of my testimony with him. Sister Josephine Walsh's book "God's Whistle" includes a short testimony about how God restored my daughter to me and I had considered whether or not to take a copy with me to Rome. However, I decided not to so I was quite amazed to find a copy of it in the college library. I have no idea how it got there but somebody must have read it and left a copy for the library. It was certainly providential because when Fr. Andrew read it he was deeply touched to read testimonies of how God had done wonderful things in the lives of very ordinary people.

"I've read many stories of the amazing things God has done for people but this is the first time I've met a living, walking story!" he laughed. "Tell me more." We spent many hours walking in the beautiful hills, sharing our experiences of God.

After spending Christmas with my family I flew to Warsaw where I was met by Father Andrew who took me to his parents' home for New Year. It was my first trip to Poland and I was overwhelmed by the kindness and warmth of the people. The contrast between the half-empty services in the UK and the packed churches in Poland was striking and I hope the faith of the people will withstand the new wave of consumerism that has swept the country since they joined the European Community.

Soon after my return from Poland I began to prepare for my trip to India. This was particularly exciting for me as it was my first visit and it was the place where my paternal grandmother was born. Her father served in the British Army in the days of the Raj and I had always been fascinated by India and its diverse cultures. Several Indian priests and sisters who had been with me in Nemi invited me to visit their mission stations in various parts of India and it was too good an opportunity to miss. At last I would see the country where my grandmother was born.

CHAPTER NINETEEN

The Jewel in the Crown

Do not worship any other God,
for the Lord is a jealous God
(Exodus 34:14)

I arrived in Mumbai in February 2003 and immediately fell in love with this incredible country and its enterprising people. Like most visitors, I thought of India as one large nation bursting at the seams with people, whereas in fact it is a fascinating kaleidoscope of twenty-six states, each with its own distinctive culture, customs and cuisine.

The moment I stepped out of the airport my senses were assaulted by an incredible variety of sights, smells and above all, sounds. India is the noisiest place I've visited and car horns and bicycle bells compete with bellowing oxen pulling heavy carts and a thousand voices all vying for attention. Temples painted in garish colours abound, each one dedicated to one of the thousands of gods and goddesses of Hinduism. Enormous statues, some of them alarmingly fearsome, are adorned with garlands of fresh flowers and depending upon the particular deity honoured. Growing and selling flowers is a flourishing business as each day thousands of garlands are bought for the temples. In some temples, rats are treated as sacred and thousands of them roam freely amongst the pilgrims whilst at others dozens of monkeys swarm over the ancient stones and nobody dare chase them away as they are venerated as gods. Elephants are often used in temple worship and it is common to see these ponderous giants moving slowly through the excited crowds.

Everywhere you turn in India there are people, thousands of them and just watching them was a fascinating pastime. Whole families perch precariously on motorcycles; up front Dad is driving with one small child in front, two more kids are squashed in the middle, whilst Mum is at the back, making sure nobody falls off! Few bother with safety helmets and you take your life in your hands when you travel on India's roads.

After a while I got used to being driven along country roads at breakneck speed, dodging the crater sized potholes. Often we'd see a massive truck heading straight towards us, horn blaring loudly, lights flashing dramatically and our nonchalant driver would swerve violently at the last possible moment to avoid a collision. It certainly encourages serious prayer when you're travelling!

Throughout India it is common to see people carrying all kinds of weird and wonderful burdens on their heads.

Women and small girls carry large water jars on their head with uncanny precision whilst older women are often sent out to forage for kindling for the fires, returning with enormous bundles of sticks   balanced on their heads. Men ride bicycles laden with all kinds of goods and tiny auto rickshaws overloaded with goods belch black smoke and fumes into the crowded streets. The sheer volume of traffic is staggering and congested roads are the order of the day. The miracle is that anybody manages to reach their destination at all.

India is a place of extremes, the contrast between rich and poor and ancient and modern is startling. In the middle of a run-down street where grazing cows nose through piles of rubbish and squealing pigs flee the wheels of overcrowded buses, you can suddenly come upon an internet café with gleaming new computers. For the equivalent of about ten pence you are transported to another world for a whole hour surfing the internet. When you step outside once more it's a tremendous culture shock as you rejoin the mayhem on the streets.

Whole families live out their entire lives at the side of the road, their only shelter a sheet of plastic supported on a few poles. It is a common sight each morning to see men stripped to the waist performing their ablutions or shaving at the side of the road using a piece of broken mirror to trim their beards. Women washed naked children in small washing up bowls without a second glance at the traffic rushing by. In the villages large satellite TV dishes cling incongruously to the sides of simple mud houses.

A favourite pastime of the poor is going to the cinema
where for a few rupees they can escape their humdrum
lives and lose themselves in the latest Bollywood epic.
These are mostly garish musicals with totally preposterous
plots but they are much loved by the thousands of poor
people who flock to see them and bring a little make-
believe glamour to their often wretched lives.

My family would have been horrified if they saw some of
the conditions I became accustomed to and the occasionally
dangerous situations I had to face. In Gujarat gangs of
armed bandits known as dacoits roam the hills looking for
vehicles to rob and on one trip our vehicle had to have an
armed guard as it was felt I'd make a good target for kidnap
by these bandits. One of the policemen casually informed
me; "They don't usually kill their hostages." If his words
were meant to reassure me they had the opposite effect!

On another occasion a curfew had been imposed in a
nearby town due to communal rioting and at one point I
was stranded overnight in a run-down house surrounded
by drunken gangs who had gone on the rampage. As I
listened to the mounting sounds of violence which seemed
to be coming closer by the minute, I could only pray that
the bars on my window were strong enough to withstand
a drunken mob! Needless to say, I didn't get much sleep
that night.

On another occasion, I became very ill during the night, a
victim of the dreaded 'Delhi belly,' which is par for the
course in India. After eating suspect fish I was violently
sick at three in the morning and as I crawled to the rather

primitive bathroom, I heard the sound of angry voices and gunshots close by. I was staying in the guest quarters in a parish complex in Gujarat but as it happened I was the only person in the building at that time. The parish house was close by but there were fierce dogs roaming the compound at night and I'd been warned not to set foot outside the door or the dogs would attack me!

"If you need anything just use the phone," I was told. However, the phone was out of order, I was desperately ill and to make things worse the gunshots were drawing closer! But if I stepped outside I would be savaged by the now frantic dogs. I thought it might be preferable to be shot; at least that would be quicker. "Dear Lord!" I moaned. "Did you bring me all this way just to let me die? If you are going to let me die, then please let it be quick!"

My bathroom was actually nothing more than a tiled room with a cold water tap attached to the wall and western style toilet which could only be flushed with a bucket of water. I doubted if the rusty shower head protruding from the wall had even seen so much as a drop of water and if I wanted to take a 'shower', my host left a bucket of hot water and a plastic jug outside my door each morning. By the time my host Father Rayappan brought the hot water along at six o'clock, I didn't care whether I lived or died but I begged him not to send me to the hospital. I'd seen the poor conditions there and felt that if I was going to die I'd rather it was with a degree of dignity at least! I was treated by a local doctor and after three days felt a little better.

"By the way, what was all that noise about the night I was

ill?" I asked Father Rayappan. "Who was firing guns?" "Oh that was just the tribal people," he replied. "Sometimes they brew their own alcohol and go a bit wild, looting and shooting the place up. That's why we have the dogs!"

Tribal people are the original inhabitants of India who lived there before the Aryans came from the north. They comprise a substantial minority of the population and are outside of the Hindu caste system. Many of them have converted to Christianity. I hoped they weren't amongst those toting the guns that night! Gujarat, the birthplace of Mahatma Gandhi, is a 'dry' state and it's illegal to sell alcohol hence the 'home brewing' of the tribal people. Not for the first time I was glad my children couldn't see where their mother was staying!

It was in Gujarat that I saw a sight which has haunted me ever since. As we driving by in our air-conditioned jeep, I glanced out of the window at a group of children who were scavenging on a rubbish tip. One of them, a little boy of no more than four years old was busy scraping scraps of food from aluminium containers – thrown out by the nearby restaurant.

"Please, can't we stop?" I cried. I wanted to help these poor children in some way. "No, Margaret, we can't. If we do we'll be mobbed and it could be dangerous" said my companion. "Well there must be something I can do to help?"

I was then told about the scheme run by the SVDs throughout India wherever they have a community. The priests build hostels to house the poorest children, usually orphans, and educate them as well as teach them useful skills such as carpentry or needlework. They have developed a system of sponsorship whereby people can sponsor a child for a certain amount of money each year to cover the costs of hostel accommodation and education.

I determined that I would make people aware of this scheme when I returned home and attempt to raise funds for this purpose. In fact people were incredibly generous when I told them about these poor children and we now have a good number of children who are sponsored in this way. Each child who is educated has a better chance to escape the vicious cycle of poverty and it is a cause that is very dear to my heart.

Indian railways are an experience not to be missed. Hundreds of people pack the platforms, many sleeping on the filthy floor, oblivious to the noisy crowds. Dozens of emaciated cows wander freely, scavenging amongst the rubbish and nobody would dare try to chase them away.

"Chai! Hot chai!" is the cry of the chai wallahs as they dart amongst the crowds with their cans of hot, sweet, milky tea. Porters with red turbans pile suitcases on their heads and it's a race to keep up with them as they scurry along on stick thin legs to find the assigned compartment. Once on board it's like entering another world. Whole families cram into tiny compartments with all manner of luggage and parcels of food for the journey, often wrapped in banana leaves to keep it fresh and moist.

The generosity of strangers on the trains was astonishing and many times families happily shared their meals with me. I was on the receiving end of much kindness and of course was often the object of much curiosity, especially in the more remote areas. I found this curiosity to be an endearing trait although it is a little disconcerting at first. People have no hesitation in asking very personal questions five minutes after meeting you. The first question is "Where are you from?" followed by "Are you married? How many children do you have? Are they settled?" – meaning are they married and do they have good jobs? They just stop short of asking for details of your annual income! But when you realise they are genuinely interested, it's impossible to take offence.

Something else which surprised me was the fondness with which the older people spoke of British rule in India. I never experienced any hostility or resentment which I had half expected from a people who were formerly subjects of a colonial power which was not always benevolent. In fact throughout India people would proudly point out various legacies of British rule such as the road and rail network and the criminal justice system. I was shocked to hear some of the older people who even went so far as to say they were sorry the British left – which is a sad indictment on their present living conditions. "There is so much corruption madam" said one old man sadly. "Everywhere it's bribery. If you can't pay, you will not get a job" said another.

Being on a train is like being in a crowded market as vendors scurry through the carriages selling everything from tea, coffee, tomato soup, curries and food of all kinds to watches, radios and digital cameras. In addition men offering Indian head massage plied their trade throughout the train but having seen one very vigorous practitioner in action, I decided to forgo that treat!

Another exotic feature of train travel was provided by the transvestites who wandered through the carriages demanding alms. Many of these men were eunuchs who had been emasculated when they were children in order that they may earn a living begging. Dressed in garish saris, wearing heavy makeup they present a rather sad sight. Apparently they are often employed to dance and entertain at weddings and there is much superstition surrounding them. Many people are afraid they'll be cursed if they refuse to give them money. Train journeys in India may be long and slow but they are certainly not dull!

On long journeys when I may spend two or three nights on the train, I usually travelled in what was known as three-tier A/C. This is an air-conditioned compartment with three bunks on each side facing each other, making a total of six sleeping berths and it was rather a shock the first time I made an overnight journey to discover that I was expected to sleep with a group of strangers, all of them men! Looking rather anxiously around me, I asked my companion Father Rayappan where we were supposed to sleep. He looked puzzled. "Why here of course, on the bunks" he said. "Don't worry, the porter will bring us a blanket and pillow." I looked aghast; blankets and pillows were the least of my worries. "What, with all these strange men?" I was horrified. I was the only woman in the whole compartment. Father Rayappan smiled and shrugged: "Margaret, this is India!"

I spent a rather anxious night as I'd been warned that I must keep my valuables with me at all times, preferably using them as a pillow! If only my friends could see me now I thought grimly as I visited the primitive toilets. The floor was so disgusting that I had no alternative but to clasp my handbag firmly in my teeth! As the train lurched round a bend I sighed and thought: "So much for exotic foreign travel. I wonder if Michael Palin has as much fun?

Trains can be very dangerous places, especially for foreigners. In Bihar which is a notoriously lawless state, the passengers on a train were robbed at gunpoint which was bad enough. But when I read that the robbers were the railway police who were supposed to be guarding them I was relieved that I hadn't been on that particular train!

Despite the widespread poverty throughout India, there is an overwhelming sense of optimism and even the poorest people seem able to find something to look forward to or celebrate. Ladies in gorgeous and immaculately clean saris step out of the most squalid mud huts and the people are often lively and exuberant despite their material poverty. Whilst I would never romanticise poverty, there is no doubt that happiness is not synonymous with wealth nor is generosity, as some of the poorest of people were willing to share what little they had with a stranger.

CHAPTER TWENTY

The Lord Provides

The Lord protects the stranger …
(Psalm 146: 9)

During my time in India I learned to appreciate many of the things I take so much for granted at home such as electricity and running water which were not always available in the places I stayed in. I learned how to make one bucket of water go a long way! It had to be carefully rationed; first I washed myself and then my clothes then finally I used it to water the plants!

Electricity was not always available either as it was rationed in some states where power cuts were a feature of everyday life. I was blessed to be able to travel the length and breadth of the country; from the Himalayas in the north down to Kanyakumari, the southernmost tip of India. I usually stayed in parish houses and convents along the way.

During the very first Mass I attended in a small convent chapel I was encouraged when I heard the words of Psalm 146:9: 'The Lord protects the stranger, and keeps the orphan and the widow.' These words rang true as I shared a delicious breakfast with the sisters who certainly made this widowed stranger welcome!

God's providence often appears in the most unexpected quarters. Over the years since I have been visiting Gujarat, I have become friendly with a Hindu businessman whose children attend the school where my friend Father Rayappan is the Principle. This man does not speak a word of English and his daughter translated our conversations. Despite this drawback, a friendship sprang up between us and he has been very kind to me, often putting his car and driver at my disposal and inviting me to his home where his wife prepares delicious meals. He is a wealthy man and lives in a beautiful home where meals are taken seated on the floor; however, although the family use their fingers to eat, thankfully cutlery was provided for me. I am pretty adaptable but I draw the line at eating curry and rice with my fingers!

This businessman has always shown me immense kindness and generosity and Father Rayappan explained that although he's Hindu, he respects the fact that I am a committed Christian who tries to share the gospel whenever I have the opportunity. He was disappointed because I was unable to return to India last year to attend his oldest daughter's wedding. Because he owns several carpet factories I nicknamed him 'Carpet Wallah,' a name which apparently delighted him.

On one occasion I was in Rajasthan in January when it can be surprisingly cold. 'Carpet Wallah' had arranged for me to stay in a hotel owned by one of his friends and when he heard that I was feeling cold at nights, he kindly arranged to have several beautiful blankets delivered to my room. I see this as evidence of God's love and provision and it often comes via unexpected sources!

Speaking of God's provision, if we are sensitive to the promptings of the Spirit, He will use us to bless others. I am reminded of the time when I visited a mission station in central India. Before leaving my home I'd packed a small Benedictine Crucifix in my case; I just had a feeling that I was to give it to somebody in India. Sure enough, after travelling to a remote outstation, I discovered the very person who needed the crucifix.

Father William a dedicated SVD priest had shown me around the compound housing a tiny school for poor tribal children and the little chapel where he said Mass each day. He was justifiably proud of what the SVDs were providing for these poor children who would otherwise have been destined to spend their lives labouring in the fields or working on the roads for a mere pittance.

After we had prayed for a time in the chapel, Fr. William reached into his cassock and pulled out a broken Benedictine Crucifix. He told me rather sadly that he'd bought it in Subeaco in Italy many years ago and was so disappointed that the figure of Christ was broken. He said that he was hoping that one day he'd be able to get a replacement. I didn't say anything to him until we got outside, when I handed him the spare one I'd brought from home. The delight on his face was a joy to behold and we both shed a tear as we reflected on God's amazing goodness and how He knows all of our needs before we even ask Him! Such incidents, whilst relatively minor, continue to remind me of the importance of listening to that 'still small voice' within which prompts us to do things which do not always make sense at the time.

I remembered an occasion when I was in Bosnia when I'd felt prompted to put an extra film in my backpack, even though I'd just loaded a fresh film into my camera that morning. When we visited a refugee camp, one of the refugees had a camera but no film and he wanted to take photos of his grandchild's forthcoming baptism. When I handed him the spare film I'd packed in my bag, tears filled his eyes, it was the very film he needed and his enthusiastic hug almost crushed my ribs! Such a small thing, but it meant so much to this man and his family. I believe the Lord prompted me to put that film in my bag that morning because He knew exactly who it was meant for.

People often ask me how I first became involved in public speaking. It was actually during my first visit to India that I was invited to share my story in public. I was in a local parish church in Gujarat which is a hotbed of Hindu fundamentalism and the site of a lot of communal violence. Although I would not normally be allowed to speak openly about Christianity in a public setting, because it was a Catholic Church and the people were already Christians, the authorities could not object; otherwise I would have been accused of trying to convert Hindus and things could become difficult for the local church.

I was invited to give my testimony after each mass and as there were four masses that day it was quite an introduction to public speaking! The first mass was in Hindi, the second in English, the third in Gujarati and the fourth in Konkani – the language of Goa (there was a large Goan population in the parish). Obviously I had to speak through an interpreter for three of the masses and although I had spoken previously to a small group in Hungary through a translator, it was quite daunting to gaze out upon hundreds of expectant faces who didn't understand a word of English.

As I stood on the altar in the early morning heat with an old fashioned fan whirring madly overhead, I could only marvel at how God could bring a housewife from Aberdeen all the way to India to witness to His love. As the day progressed, the heat intensified and despite the many ceiling fans whirling around somewhat shakily, the sweat was pouring from me and I was relieved when the final talk ended. All in all it was a wonderful learning experience for me, and one that would stand me in good stead in the future as God led me to even more unusual settings to share my testimony and speak about His mercy.

It is always a great privilege to be invited to witness to God's love and I had to be ready and willing to speak at the drop of a hat in a variety of different settings. At first I was terrified as I faced dozens of strangers, especially in such a different culture. I know that I could never have done it in my own strength so I had to rely totally on the Lord to inspire me. He never failed me, and once I began to speak, the fear left me as I focused on the Lord and His goodness.

I try to emphasise God's love and mercy and the fact that He never gives up on us but pursues us until He can finally get our attention. This often happens of course when we find ourselves in great difficulty, as I did. The whole point is that what God did for me He will do for others and if I can give one person hope in a difficult situation then I am happy to share my experiences. For instance, people often approach me after a talk and confide that either they or somebody in their family has a problem with alcohol. I am able to give them practical suggestions as to where they might get help as well as pray for them.

The church in India seems to have a degree of freedom lacking in the west and I didn't always know when I would be called upon to speak. For instance, I might be sitting quietly at mass when the priest would catch my eye and beckon me up onto the altar and invite me to share my story without any previous warning. This might not be orthodox but who am I to argue when I am generously invited to share the Good News? They are obviously not so bound by rules and regulations.

The settings varied enormously too. Sometimes I might find myself addressing large crowds in a magnificent cathedral and the next day I might find myself in a tiny village church which was actually no more than three low walls and a grass roof supported on bamboo poles, with a plastic table forming the altar. Often the ground in such churches was terribly uneven and the 'altar' was propped up with stones!

In one such village in Andhra Pradesh, a small Pentecostal Church had recently opened and an unfortunate rivalry had sprung up between this group and the local Catholics. Father James said Mass there once a week in the evening and he warned me, "As soon as they hear us, they'll start making a lot of noise!" Sure enough, as soon as Mass began, the sound of drums and loud music shattered the night air. It was a case of who could make the most noise! I was saddened by this situation which I felt was a poor witness of Christian unity to the local Hindus. Father James had tried to befriend the pastor, who unfortunately was adamant that Catholics are not true Christians but rather "rely on the works of the flesh for salvation instead of the blood of Jesus," as this particular pastor put it.

Fr. James suspected that the pastor had been taught this by wealthy American evangelicals who came into the area and funded new churches. Sadly when they returned to the States, which they usually did after only a short time, they often left behind situations of bitterness, rivalry and hostility between their converts and the local Catholics. Thankfully Fr. James in his wisdom insists that his little congregation do not retaliate but instead pray for those who cause them problems and continue to extend the hand of friendship despite the hostility.

The congregations in the villages in Andhra Pradesh where Fr. James serves are mostly made up of poor day labourers and their families. Men, women and children of all ages sit cross-legged on the ground during Mass in an attitude of deep reverence and I was greatly impressed by their simple faith and generosity. Despite their own obvious poverty they wanted to support the work of Fr. James and were eager to become involved in parish work such as catechetics. They were also determined to build a new church to replace the rather ramshackle building that serves as a church.

After one of my trips my parish generously took up a collection and the money was used by Fr. James to buy a dozen new bicycles to enable the faithful catechists to travel from village to village. Fr. James sent us some delightful photos of a ceremony he had conducted to bless and commission both the catechists and their shiny new bicycles!

After mass there was invariably an excited group of people who insisted on placing a garland of flowers around my neck. Then somebody was dispatched to fetch tea and biscuits for 'Madam'. I felt deeply humbled by their generosity, especially as I have so much compared to the little that these people have.

I soon discovered that the villagers were hungry for the Word of God and as they were delightfully unsophisticated it was a challenge for me to ensure my talks were relevant within the context of their everyday lives. It was easy to see why Jesus who was such a wonderful storyteller drew on nature to illustrate His parables.

One day I was sharing my testimony in a tiny village church packed with labourers who worked in the paddy fields. The men sat solemnly on one side of the church and the ladies in their colourful saris sat on the opposite side.

Several of the young men perched precariously on the window ledges and I hoped that none of them would fall asleep and fall from the window like the youth described in the Book of Acts (Acts 20:9-10) as unlike St. Paul, I didn't feel able to raise anybody from the dead! I wanted to share with these villagers how my faith had come alive and I often describe myself as a 'submarine Catholic,' somebody who surfaced once a week at Sunday Mass and spent the rest of the week 'submerged.' However I was pretty sure that the villagers wouldn't have a clue what a submarine was.

As I looked at the little congregation I had a sudden inspiration. Earlier that morning I had watched fascinated as a man had driven his herd of water buffaloes into a large pond for their daily 'wash and brush up'. Soon the animals were completely submerged and the only part of them that was visible was their nostrils and so I told the people that I used to be a water buffalo Catholic and moments later their faces were wreathed in smiles as it dawned on them what I meant.

I discovered that many people in India are multi-lingual. Apart from the language of their native state, priests and sisters for example would have to learn Hindi which is the national language, as well as English and the language of whatever state they happened to be working in. In addition, there are various tribal languages and dialects to be mastered too. My host, Father James told me that he enjoyed translating my talks as he never knew what I was going to say next. Often he would have to wait until he'd stopped laughing before he could continue in the local dialect and sometimes he struggled to find the appropriate

word. He is a native of Kerala and so his first language
is Malayalam, and although he is fluent in Telegu, the
language of Andhra Pradesh, at times he couldn't
immediately remember the correct word in the local
dialect.

On one such occasion, the Lord Himself helped out. I'd
been speaking about transformation in Christ and how our
lives can be likened to a caterpillar which eventually
becomes a beautiful butterfly. Whilst Father James was
struggling to recall the local word for butterfly, a gasp rose
from the crowd. A breathtakingly beautiful butterfly had
suddenly appeared in the church and as this was night time
it was a most unusual sight. The people were even more
surprised when Father James finally managed to translate
what I'd just been saying. We agreed afterwards that the
Lord is indeed gracious and wonderful!

"They won't forget that moment Margaret. The memory of
that butterfly and your message will stay with them."
Once again I felt privileged to be asked to share the gospel
with people who were so receptive and my faith was given
a boost too.

On another occasion I was invited to speak to a group of
villagers in a remote area as they were settling down to
watch a play performed by a group of travelling actors. I
had no idea what the play was about, except that it was
based on a Gospel story. It was pitch dark and the only
lights were provided by flickering oil lamps set up on poles
in a small clearing. Although it was evening, it was still hot
and as I looked out at the sea of expectant faces the sweat
was pouring from me.

It was not the most comfortable place to do a talk and I wasn't even sure what I was going to say! I knew that the people earned their meagre living working in the paddy fields and tending the landowner's crops. The ladies were wearing their best saris and the men had obviously put on their cleanest shirts and even the little children seemed to be wearing their best clothes. This was obviously a big night out for them and they gazed at me expectantly. After a quick prayer, I felt prompted to talk to them about the 'Parable of the Sower' (Matthew 13:1-23) as I knew they would understand only too well the importance of having the right conditions for sowing seed and what happens when conditions are not poor.

It must have been divine inspiration because after I had finished speaking, the Sister who was producing the play approached me. "I don't believe it," she said. "How did you know what we were doing?" I was mystified and she went on to say that the name of that night's production was: "A man went out to sow …" based of course on the story in Matthew's gospel. God is indeed extraordinary and inspires us if we will learn to listen to that still small voice. I wish I could say I always listen, but of course I don't!

On another occasion in Kerala, I attended a small house group where we'd shared the gospel and after the meeting I was asked to pray with people. Just as we were getting ready to say a closing prayer, a shy young face peered around the door and after much whispering, a young girl came into the room. It was one of the house servants and as she was a Hindu I was surprised when I was asked to pray with her. Through a translator I explained that I would be praying for her to Jesus if she was agreeable and she happily nodded her head.

As I prayed, a picture came into my mind of the girl with a badly beaten face and I received a word of knowledge to the effect that her father was in the habit of beating her. Trying to be tactful, I enquired about the girl's relationship with her father and she immediately began to weep. When I described the picture I'd seen she was astonished and wanted to know how I could possibly know that her father did indeed beat both her and her mother when he was drunk. I told her that Jesus showed me this because he loves her and her family, including her abusive father. She said she loved him too and it was only when he had been drinking that he abused his family. After a brief prayer when I asked the Lord to heal this girl and her mother, I asked if she was willing to forgive her father and she readily agreed. I prayed for him to be released from his addiction to alcohol and for peace to be restored to their home. When the girl left the room she was much happier than when she came in. I don't know the outcome of that story; I must leave that in the Lord's hands. But it was a lesson as to how Jesus truly does love all people and how His gospel overcomes cultural and religious boundaries.

I often found myself in some unexpected and challenging situations in India. I was in Andhra Pradesh one February when my visit happened to coincide with the feast of Our Lady of Lourdes. In that state the feast is traditionally celebrated at the shrine of Our Lady in Vijayawada with it's replica of the Lourdes Grotto. Vijayawada is a large city and the home of the Diocesan Pastoral Centre; scores of priests and sisters gather there for the annual celebration of the feast day, together with thousands of Catholics, Hindus and Moslems who gather to share and enjoy the festive atmosphere. Celebrations are spread over three days and people travel for hundreds of miles to be there. The high point of the three day gathering is the final Mass, concelebrated by several bishops and dozens of priests.

The local bishop who is a great supporter of Charismatic Renewal invited me to share my testimony at the conclusion of the Mass and I happily agreed. However nobody mentioned just how many people would be present and as I gazed out across the sea of faces I was overwhelmed by the sheer numbers. I was told later that around fifty thousand people were present! The Lord certainly has a sense of humour: had I known what to expect I would have been terrified. But I was touched by the warmth of the people and their receptiveness to my message about God's love.

Next day, at the railway station, I was approached by two young men who didn't speak English but who wanted to shake my hand. It turned out that they had been present at the Mass and apparently they thought I was a famous American evangelist who appears on TV! I was glad they hadn't asked for my autograph, they would have been disappointed!

Another occasion when I was taken by surprise occurred in Chennai (formerly Madras) the capital city of Tamil Nadu. I was staying in a convent on St. Thomas Mount where St. Thomas the Apostle is reputed to have spent some time and one evening after supper, I was asked if I would do a talk in the nearby seminary. I agreed thinking they meant the following day but was shocked to learn that I had exactly one hour to prepare! Mindful of Jesus' words: 'Without me you can do nothing' (John 15:5), I hurried off to the chapel to pray and seek guidance. As I prayed, the words 'Isaiah 29 verse 13' came to mind and I quickly picked up my bible to check it out. I was horrified to discover that it was an admonition from God, accusing the people of worshipping him with their lips only whilst their hearts were far from him!

"Lord!" I said. "Who am I to come into a seminary with a message like that? I don't even know them and they might think I'm criticising them!"

The Lord gently reminded me that I too had worshipped Him with my lips only for most of my life. It was only His grace and the power of the Holy Spirit which had changed my worship from being merely an outward form of religion into something more meaningful. I recalled the words of philosopher Martin Buber who said: "Nothing so obscures the face of God as religion."

I felt terribly nervous as I stood before a large group of keen and curious young seminarians and to my acute anxiety I noticed a group of professors standing with arms folded at the back of the hall! Although right then I felt like running away, there was no escape. I find the best way of sharing my story is to simply be myself and not try to impress anybody. The minute I do otherwise I fall flat on my face! So, trying to not to feel too intimidated by these learned professors, I shared my testimony as simply and honestly as possible.

I believe that God wants us to have an intimate relationship with him and not just practice a lifeless form of religion. Many of us think this is an impossible ideal which only saints can achieve but we often forget that saints are in fact ordinary people who are enabled by the grace of God to do extraordinary things. Because they are conscious of their weakness, God is able to manifest His power through them.

In his letter to the Philippians, Paul says: "I am no longer trying for perfection by my own efforts, the perfection that comes from the law, but I want only the perfection that comes through faith in Christ, and is from God and based on faith" (Phil 3:9). For so many years I had tried to be 'good' by carrying out religious practices, and had failed miserably. I know now that I cannot achieve holiness, all I can do is yield to the action of the Holy Spirit in my life and leave the rest to Him.

As I looked at these eager young men I was struck by how much influence for good or ill they would have in the future in the parishes they would be sent to and I reminded them they would have many opportunities to help their parishioners develop spiritual gifts. After all, whilst priests have a unique calling, every baptised person has a duty and responsibility to serve the Lord in whatever capacity they can and I hoped that seeing what God can do with a very ordinary housewife might encourage them! Hopefully the days of a two-tier church consisting of ordained and religious who serve God and those who are merely spectators is disappearing.

Thankfully the talk was well received and several of the

professors thanked me afterwards for helping to bring to life the fact that Jesus did indeed come for sinners and not the 'righteous.' I am in no doubt which category I belong to, and that in itself is only through the grace of God. On the flight home I reflected on what an amazing God we have.

If we are willing, God will use us in the most unexpected ways. I thought back to the times when I had contemplated suicide because I had felt so useless. As I looked at my rather battered bible, I remembered how it had come into my possession and how there was a time when I preferred to spend my money on alcohol rather than the bible. I could never have imagined during the days when I lay in an alcoholic stupor that one day I would be standing in a remote village in India sharing the Gospel with hundreds of people or speaking to seminarians about the love and mercy of God. It was not long before the Lord led me to even more exotic locations.

CHAPTER TWENTY-ONE

Come Fly With Me

The Lord will guide you always;
He will satisfy your needs
in a sun-scorched land
(Isaiah 58: 11)

After spending some time with the family, I packed my case once more and headed off this time for the wilds of Papua New Guinea – more commonly referred to as 'PNG.' Father Janusz, a Polish priest I'd met in Nemi had invited me to visit him at his large parish in the Wewak Diocese of Papua New Guinea and en-route I stopped off in Singapore where I did some sightseeing.

One of the most popular tourist haunts is the legendary Raffles Hotel where one is traditionally supposed to enjoy a drink at the famous long bar. As I sipped a soft drink, I silently thanked God that I am sober these days as I dread to think what mischief I might have got up to so far from home in my drinking days! I was grateful that those days are far behind me now and my mission nowadays is quite different and does not involve finding the bar that stays open the longest!

After another stopover in Cairns Australia, I took the short flight to Port Moresby the capital of Papua New Guinea and gazed in wonder as the small plane flew low over the Great Barrier Reef. The magnificence of God's creation never fails to amaze me and as I gazed down at the clear turquoise waters where the reefs were clearly outlined, I could only marvel at the beauty whilst feeling sad that we are destroying so much of it in the pursuit of wealth. I remembered the first time I saw the Rocky Mountains in Canada; I was so overwhelmed by the majesty and beauty of those towering crags that I was reduced to tears.

After enjoying the natural splendour of the Great Barrier Reef, Port Moresby came as something of a shock. It is not a place of beauty and resembles a Wild West town during the Gold Rush rather than a capital city! Papua New Guinea is noted for its extreme lawlessness and most of it is centered in Port Moresby.

There are many unskilled labourers in the town who are paid fortnightly and on pay day they go on drunken rampages. Known locally as 'rascals' this rather jaunty name belies the viciousness of their actions and the murder rate is very high. Nothing is sacred to them when they're fuelled by alcohol and the compound of the Divine Word Missionaries where I was to stay had recently been attacked.

A group of rascals had stolen a mechanical digger which they used to flatten the surrounding fence. They then attacked the house with sticks, stones and metal bars and had the house not been heavily fortified, somebody might have been killed. The frightened priests could only stay indoors and pray that the men would give up and go home which they eventually did. But it was a nasty situation, made worse by the fact that the local police refused to come to their aid on the grounds that they had 'run out of ammunition!' This is apparently a common excuse along with: "We have no fuel for our vehicles!" The truth is, the police force are themselves intimidated by 'the rascals' and avoid taking action whenever possible.

Shortly after I left PNG, a contingent of police officers was flown in from Australia in an attempt to train the local police force and restore some semblance of law and order to the capital. I soon realised that I was in a place which exceeded normal boundaries and I would have to suspend any expectations I might have had and 'go with the flow.' Compared to Papua New Guinea, India was a 'walk in the park.'

Whilst I was visiting the university at Madang, one of the priests who was himself a native of PNG, told me a harrowing tale of a recent journey he'd made on one of the notorious public transport vehicles known as PMVs. These vehicles are not buses in the accepted sense but can be anything from an ancient VW Minibus to an open flatbed truck and travel on them is not advisable for tourists as they are frequently ambushed. The priest had been sitting next to an apparently amiable young man to whom he'd been speaking for the last hour. All of a sudden the vehicle lurched to a halt as one of the passengers pulled out a gun and held it to the driver's head. The 'amiable young man' was his accomplice and wasted no time in ordering everybody to get out and place all their valuables in a large holdall he was carrying. Not only did he rob the priest but he viciously beat him and left him for dead at the roadside. It was a senseless act of violence and a salutary warning not to travel on public transport.

After spending a few days at the Diocesan Seminary where I gave some talks to the junior seminarians, I flew in a small rickety plane to Wewak on the coast. My accommodation there was rather primitive and although it was situated in a compound, I was given an escort to and from my room as there was a high risk that I would be robbed if I was unaccompanied.

One night I was woken up by a tremendous storm and as there was no glass in the windows, the torrential rain lashed my face and soon soaked my bed! The Hilton it most definitely was not! Whoever thinks travelling to exotic locations must be wonderful should have a chat with me sometime! Although the storm eventually died down, it was anything but peaceful. Hundreds of large noisy frogs had taken refuge under the house where I was staying and had it not been for the earplugs without which I never travel, sleep would have been impossible.

I first realised the value of earplugs when I was in Jerusalem some years ago. Our hotel was situated close to a mosque where the early morning call to prayer was ear shattering.

Also, the hotel room had no curtains, just a flimsy voile drape and so another essential travel item is a sleep mask!

The morning after the torrential downpour, the priests commented on the fact that the storm was 'fairly mild' and reminded me that some years previously the island had been battered by a tsunami when more than two thousand people lost their lives. I'm glad I live in a country where the climate is fairly stable and reflected on the fact that it's usually the poorest nations who suffer the effects of extreme weather conditions.

My friend Father Janusz finally arrived from the bush to collect me and after loading his pickup truck with huge drums of diesel and boxes of provisions we headed out to the bush. After several hours of driving on badly potholed roads, the tarmac petered out and became a rutted track through the bush. When I told Father Janusz that I needed a 'comfort stop,' he laughed and warned me to be very careful as there are many deadly snakes in PNG. Needless to say, I made a very quick and nervous trip into the bush. This reminded me of a similar occasion in India, but in addition to snakes, I was warned not to wander too far as a tiger had been sighted in the vicinity!

The journey from Wewak took around six hours and I was grateful that the pickup truck at least had air-conditioning, even if the suspension was pretty basic. Although Father Janusz lives in quite a large house with several spare bedrooms, despite my advancing years, it would have scandalised the people if I'd stayed there alone with him and so it was agreed that I should stay with the small community of Sisters. Their convent was little more than a large corrugated shed, divided into a number of rooms. There was no electricity in the bush and I ruefully put my hairdryer and travel kettle back in my case. I learned to appreciate the noisy old generator which at least provided power for a couple of hours each night.

My bed was a high old hospital bed with a metal frame and I was glad of this when I saw the number of cockroaches scuttling around my room. The first night when I got up during the night I stepped unsuspectingly on a large number of them in my bare feet and when I hastily put my slippers on, I realised the cockroaches had found a cosy nest! In future I made sure I slept with my slippers under my pillow each night and if I needed to get up during the night I rattled the bedpost to give the cockroaches advance warning so they could run and hide! There is no phone out in the bush and as bush radio is the only means of communication, I could only hope that no emergencies arose back home as I couldn't use my mobile phone either.

People in PNG are rather unconventional to say the least and the rules of the religious houses are obviously more relaxed than in the West. On the first morning when I opened my curtains I was startled to see one of the nuns leisurely scattering feed for the chickens with a cigarette dangling from her lips! It was certainly different from the more sedate convents I was used to staying in but despite their rather unorthodox lifestyle, they were devout women who served God in the poorest of the poor. They were very kind to me and welcomed me graciously into their humble home.

As we were so far out in the bush, obtaining fresh food was something of a problem and after a month of eating mainly rice, dried biscuits, tinned corned beef and noodles, I was glad to get back into town where at least there was fish and chicken available. As potatoes are only grown in the Highland region of Papua New Guinea and were not available on the coast, I really appreciated the humble spud and when I got back home my first request was for bangers and mash!

If I have learned one thing on my travels it is that all preconceived notions have to be discarded and what is acceptable behaviour in Europe is often not the norm in other cultures. I had to quickly learn to put aside my prejudices and notions of what is 'nice behaviour' if I was to survive and I certainly found Papua New Guinea to be particularly challenging in this respect

The first Sunday Mass I attended in Fr. Janusz's parish was an unforgettable experience. After spending a few moments in quiet prayer I opened my eyes and was startled to see a wild eyed man staring at me. It was all the more startling because he was stark naked! Not quite what I was used to at Sunday morning mass and I had to laugh as I imagined the shocked reactions of some of our more staid parishioners back home! Having just got over that shock I was jostled by a large dog which ran past me with another even larger dog in hot pursuit. Chickens wandered freely up and down the aisles throughout Mass, clucking loudly and leaving their natural 'deposits' throughout the church. I decided there was nothing for it but to just accept that that's how they did things here and concentrate on the mass as best I could.

I was soon hemmed in by a large curious crowd and I realised that as in India, the idea of personal space was non-existent and I'd just have to get used to the rather pungent smell of people who definitely do not like bathing!

Another favourite pastime during Mass was checking each other's heads for lice and killing the offending creatures, crushing them with a loud crack on their fingernails! Nose-picking was another socially acceptable habit, and I soon learned that it was better to focus on what was taking place on the altar rather than my neighbours' personal habits!

Mass got underway and as it was conducted in the local language, Pidgin English, it was challenging trying to decipher the rather strange words. After a while I found that I could actually understand some of it. It's a very phonetic language, for instance, Tok bilong God means The Word of God – which makes sense if you think about it; and Umi Pray is simply Let us Pray.

Mass was a very colourful affair and what the people lacked in sophistication they more than made up for in enthusiasm. I was fascinated to watch the offertory procession as women in grass skirts and very little else carried yams and sweet potatoes to the altar. Fierce looking men with painted faces blew on reed instruments or banged drums as they followed the women down the aisle. Rather than have a collection basket passed around, each person walked up to the altar and placed whatever they could afford in a basket. Some brought produce such as fruit whilst others put in small coins. It was very important to them that each person went to the altar to make their personal offering to God.

Mass lasted for over two hours and Father Janusz told me later that if he tried to shorten it, the people - many of whom had walked miles through the jungle to attend - would feel cheated. Sunday was the highlight of their week and after Mass they sat in sociable groups in the shade catching up on the local gossip and eating a picnic lunch, wrapped in banana leaves which both kept the food moist and acted as a plate; very practical.

Father Janusz invited me to conduct a three day retreat for local teachers in the parish which called upon all my powers of invention! For a start this was the first time I had ever been asked to lead a retreat and trying to offer something which was culturally relevant was a challenge to say the least. The concept of forgiveness is alien to the people in Papua New Guinea as they have a culture of 'pay back,' which is very similar to the Old Testament idea of an eye for an eye and a tooth for a tooth and revenge is a way of life for them. However, after I spoke on the importance of forgiveness and how Jesus emphasises the need to pray for our enemies, through the grace of God, many in the parish were reconciled and old grievances were laid to rest and there were tears as they embraced each other. It is very humbling to see the Lord touch people's hearts in this way and I could only stand back in amazement as many hurts were healed simply by their willingness to forgive.

One of the scriptures I used was Luke 19 – the story of Jesus' encounter with Zacchaeus, the despised tax collector. I asked the participants to imagine themselves in the tree when the Lord passes by and calls out their name. How did they feel? What did Jesus say to them? This was the first time they had ever attempted such an exercise and it presented them with a whole new way of approaching the gospels.

One of the retreatants had recently started attending a newly opened Seventh Day Adventist mission and was now highly critical of Catholicism. He approached me some days later and told me that I was the first 'born again Catholic' that he'd ever met and this had made quite an impression on him. I was deeply touched when he presented me with 20 kinas (about three pounds) which represented a lot of money for him. He said that he and his wife had prayed about this and they felt the Lord wanted them to give me this money 'for your mission.' I still have that money today as a reminder of the generosity of that poor man and his wife.

There was much laughter during this retreat too and I remember one incident in particular. During a tea break I was walking over to the refreshment tent with some of the retreatants when I happened to glance up at a coconut tree which I noticed was laden with tender green coconuts. I jokingly asked who was going to climb the tree and get me one of the delicious coconuts when suddenly there was a loud thud as a large green coconut fell at my feet! There was an excited buzz and the people were astonished; coconuts do not generally fall when they are green and they insisted that God had sent me the coconut!

"You told us that God provides for you when you travel. Now we see what you mean!" they told me excitedly. "You'll never convince them that God didn't send you that coconut!" laughed Father Janusz. "From now on you'll be known as the miracle woman!" As for me, I was convinced it was a miracle that the coconut had not hit me on the head and killed me as the trees are around thirty feet high!

After the retreat, I visited several out-stations with Father Janusz which involved a trip into the bush on roads which were little more than rutted tracks. In the rainy season these become impassable so Father Janusz has to make as many trips as possible during the dry season. Bridges in PNG are often very rudimentary affairs and at one point all Father Janusz's driving skills were called into play as he carefully drove the pickup truck across a fast flowing river on a bridge which was reduced to two planks! The rest of the bridge had been 'borrowed' by locals making repairs to their houses and I made that crossing with eyes tightly closed and a desperate prayer!

"You see Margaret; the people here don't worry about tomorrow and the fact that they might need a bridge in an emergency. They just think about their immediate needs so if they need wood for a fire or some building project, they just chop up the bridge!" When we reached the end of the track we could take the truck no further and had to walk through dense bush until we reached the village. Again we had to cross a fast flowing river but this time there was just one narrow plank left to walk on! "Do you think you can manage Margaret?" Janusz said rather doubtfully. "Well, I'll give it a try" I said. I didn't have much choice really. We decided that Janusz would go first and I would follow slowly, clinging desperately to his rucksack. And in this fashion we managed to make the crossing.

"Please Lord," I whispered, "no more of these bridges!" I have no doubt that the Lord has a sense of humour and I am sure He smiled as I gingerly hung on for dear life to Fr. Janusz. Jesus did tell us that "It is a narrow path that leads to life" (Matt 7:14) but he forgot to warn us about the bridges in Papua New Guinea!

A welcoming party was awaiting us and the villagers garlanded us with flowers. They were delighted to have the opportunity to attend Mass and I thought of how we take Mass for granted at home and perhaps do not appreciate it as we would if we could only attend occasionally. Mass was celebrated in an open sided thatched mud hut and the altar had been hand carved from a large log. The people of PNG are noted for their exquisite wood carvings, particularly their 'story boards' which depict the history of the local community. I was presented with one before I left but unfortunately I could not bring it home with me as I was spending a month in Australia next and Australian Customs will not allow you to bring these items into the country for fear of contamination.

Another essential item in PNG is the bilum which is a bag traditionally woven from bark but now more often made from nylon or string. You cannot be without a bilum as they hold everything needed for the day and come in all shapes and sizes. Men and women carry them and the smaller ones are draped around the forehead whilst the bigger ones are slung over the shoulder. Different patterns are used which identify the particular region they were made in and they are often extraordinarily beautiful.

The altar although simple was skillfully crafted showing scenes from the life of Christ and was covered by a cloth woven from bark. The usual offerings of yams, sweet potatoes, and bananas were placed around the altar at the offertory and it was humbling to see with what reverence they were laid down. As Mass can only be celebrated infrequently, it is a very special occasion when the priest visits and the whole village had turned out. I compared this with our Masses at home which are often attended grudgingly with parishioners looking at their watches and complaining if the sermon is too long! Afterwards, we were seated at a table in the shade of a large tree and served a delicious meal which had been cooking in the ground during Mass it was served piping hot, wrapped in banana leaves and certainly made a change from the usual tea and biscuits we have back home in the parish hall!

We had to leave in time to make the hazardous crossing on the plank bridges before dusk or run the risk of becoming crocodile fodder! One can only admire the tremendous dedication with which priests such as Father Janusz and his confreres serve the people in such difficult and dangerous situations.

I had another interesting excursion when I was invited to accompany one of the nuns who was taking medical supplies to several out-stations upriver. This involved a week long trip up the Sepik River in a small boat and we would stay in a different mission station each night. It was an exciting prospect and a once in a lifetime opportunity to meet people who until relatively recently had been cannibals and head hunters. I almost changed my mind when I saw how small the 'boat' actually was, it was just a large canoe really with an outboard motor and the boatman was a fierce looking character called Samuel. For the next week our lives were going to be pretty much in his hands.

As there was no shade on the boat, I had to spend most of the day with my head swathed in an assortment of hats and towels to protect myself from the fierce sun. A large flowery umbrella completed the ensemble and I must have presented a bizarre sight to the astonished villagers who lined the river bank. Once we were spotted, a shout would go up and dozens of villagers left what they were doing to stare at the strange vision slowly floating by.

Despite the primitive conditions on the boat, the only thing that really worried me was the mosquitoes for which the Sepik is notorious. "You'll be eaten alive!" I'd been warned. "When you swipe the mosquitoes off, your arm will be a mass of blood" another cheerful soul assured me. I prayed the Lord would protect me because despite the drugs I was taking, I knew there was still a high risk of contracting malaria in this part of the world. This was something I dreaded as I know that once in your system, malaria can be a persistently recurring problem.

For the whole of the time I was on that river I never saw one mosquito! It was unbelievable but wherever we went, people remarked on the absence of these tiny insects which cause such havoc. Father Janusz assured me that in all his years in PNG he'd never travelled on the Sepik without being badly bitten by mosquitoes. I was told later that as soon as we went back to the town, the mosquitoes descended in their thousands! Later I thanked God for his providence when I read the words in Isaiah: "The Lord will guide you always; he will satisfy your needs in a sun-scorched land and will strengthen your frame." (Is.58:11). He had certainly taken care of my needs in Papua New Guinea and kept me safe from the burning sun and mosquitoes. I wasn't too sure about the strengthening of my frame though, as I reflected wryly on my meagre diet!

One day we arrived at a village just as dusk was falling and I was surprised to hear a loud shout of "Alleluia!" as we left the boat. Our visit had coincided with a Charismatic Rally which was being held in the area and it was wonderful to see what God is doing in these remote parts of the world; to hear people loudly praising God and shouting for joy did marvels for my own faith. At times in the West our worship can be tepid and our fear of what others will think of us often inhibits our praise and worship. These people in the jungles of Papua New Guinea had no such inhibitions and their joy was obvious as they threw their spears in the air and whooped for joy!

It was exciting to see how the Lord is touching their hearts and setting them free from superstitious behaviour and occult practices. I was given a warm welcome and invited to share my testimony and once again it was humbling to see the eager faces of men and women of all ages, hungry to hear the good news of Jesus Christ. Before I went to sleep that night I thanked God for the wonderful opportunity He'd given me to share the Gospel, although it almost proved to be my last one!

That night as I returned to my room, I was stopped in my tracks by an urgent shout from Father Janusz. "Margaret, stop! Don't move another step!" he cried. I froze as I saw a small black and white snake slithering towards me. With a swift movement Father Janusz flicked the snake away with a stick. "That was a close call" he said. "Another step and you'd have been dead. That's the most deadly snake in Papua New Guinea!" I've since learned that hundreds of people die there each year because of snake bites and the lack of anti-venom serum.

The house I stayed in was very basic and as there was no bed, I slept on the floor. I was glad that it was built on stilts as at least there were no cockroaches swarming around. However, there was no plumbing either and when I asked about the bathroom, my hostess laughed and pointed out a small wooden shack at the edge of the jungle. It was an unforgettable experience, trekking across the field in the dead of night, flashes of lightning illuminating my path accompanied by the loudest thunder I've ever heard! Needless to say, mindful of the presence of snakes my nocturnal trips were made at top speed! That night as I hurried back up the rickety staircase to my room, I reflected how shocked my family would be if they saw me in these surroundings. And to think they often say: "Oh, well at least we don't have to worry about Mum on her trips; after all she can't come to much harm speaking in churches and staying with nuns!"

One day whilst we were on the river I was lazily trailing my hand in the water when Father Janusz warned that it was not a good idea as the river is infested with crocodiles and what I'd at first taken to be logs floating downstream were in fact crocodiles! Little did I think that at my age I would be travelling the world sharing the gospel and having close encounters with deadly snakes and crocodiles. But I am just an ordinary woman serving an extraordinary God and just as Jesus fed a huge crowd with a few loaves and fishes, he can use us with all our limitations; all He needs is our willingness and He will do the rest. It is often said that God does not call the equipped, but rather equips those he calls.

As my time in Papua New Guinea drew to an end I could only marvel at the wonderful work the church is doing throughout the world and when people criticise the church, I remind them that there are thousands of priests, sisters and lay people who quietly and faithfully serve the poorest of the poor without complaint, sometimes in situations of great danger.

My trip to Papua New Guinea had been interesting and unforgettable and I thanked the Lord for giving me the opportunity to see the Church at work in such a fascinating setting but I was not sorry to be going home. I was exhausted and glad to spend a month in Australia with friends, recovering from my experiences before heading back once more to my family and the comforts of home.

CHAPTER TWENTY-TWO

Spread the Good News!

Go out to the whole world;
Proclaim the Good News to all creation
(Mark 16: 15)

After spending Christmas with the family I left early in the New Year for another trip to India. This time I flew to Kerala first where I attended the wedding of a young man whose brother lives in Aberdeen. Baji was unable to attend his brother's wedding as his first child was due at that time. He asked me to represent him and as I had already planned to attend a seminar in that area, I was happy to oblige. I was treated as an honoured guest and invited to wear a sari! I must say this is a most beautiful garment and good for the posture as one has to walk very carefully to avoid falling flat on your face!

The wedding ceremony was conducted in the Syro-Malabar rite which is more elaborate and takes much longer than the

Roman rite. The celebrations continued for two days and guests were invited to a lavish feast at the bridegroom's home on the day of the wedding and another one the following day. It coincided with the annual festival held in honour of St. Sylvester, obviously a great favourite in those parts judging by the street decorations and massive firework displays held in his honour!

After the wedding I went to Ernakulam where I attended a five day conference on Healing and Deliverance. The principal speakers were Father Rufus Pereira who is well respected in the area of healing and deliverance, and Father Larry Hogan, the exorcist for the Archdiocese of Vienna. It was a most enlightening experience and I learned a lot about the reality of evil and the fact that we are indeed engaged in a spiritual battle. St. Paul reminds us: "Our struggle is not against flesh and blood … but against the powers of this dark world and against the spiritual forces of evil in the heavenly realms."

As Fr. Rufus pointed out, we cannot afford to bury our head in the sand and ignore reality just because it is not a pleasant subject. He asked us: "When was the last time you heard a sermon on Ephesians Six? Make no mistake, we are in a battle and spiritual warfare is very real. We are up against a very powerful enemy who is out to steal our peace and take us away from God. That is why we must pay heed to the words of St. Paul and put on our 'spiritual armour' every day paying special attention to what Paul refers to as 'the Sword of the Spirit' – and read the bible daily" (Eph 6:10-18). Otherwise we are at the mercy of the forces of darkness who are out to destroy us!" It was a very sobering thought and I had to agree, it is not something that is generally addressed in our parishes. But looking at the world today who can doubt the reality of an evil entity who is out to kill steal and destroy (John 10:10).

Whilst I was at the conference I was delighted to run into Fr. Sabu, who had been a fellow student on the Dei Verbum course at Nemi. India is a huge country with millions of people and the odds against us meeting like that must have been high. He told me that since returning to India he was travelling throughout the country spreading the gospel and that it was becoming more and more dangerous as the hostility of Hindu fundamentalists increased. "People in Europe don't realise Margaret just how persecuted the Church is in many parts of the world. I felt sad when I saw the empty churches in Rome and in Germany too and I wondered if Europeans would survive the fierce persecution we endure here?" I could only agree with him.

I remembered how shocked and saddened some of my fellow students had been when they saw that many of the churches in Rome appear to be little more than museums. The priests from Africa for instance had been horrified to discover that in many parishes only a handful of mostly elderly women regularly attended Mass and that indifference to spirituality seemed to be widespread. They had naively assumed that as Rome is where the Vatican is situated, faith would be lively and vibrant. Fr. Emil remarked one day: "I see now Margaret that Rome may be where the power is, but it is not where the faith is." And he described the masses celebrated in his parish back in Ghana where the people would clap and dance their way down the aisle at the offertory, and masses sometimes last for hours. "My people expect a good sermon from me and if I preached for less than forty minutes they'd be angry!" No wonder he was so shocked at the tepid faith he witnessed in Europe.

Before heading back to Mumbai I spent a week relaxing at Kovalam Beach, a popular Kerala resort. I made friends with many of the traders, who after initially pestering me to buy their goods hunkered down on the sand beside me for a chat. Like many Indians they were endearingly curious especially about a woman travelling alone and wanted to know why I was alone and what I was doing in India. I told them about the conference in Ernakulam and they were fascinated when I spoke about Jesus. Several of them shared their difficulties with me and asked me to pray with them. I quickly earned the name 'Amma Ji', a term of respect and once when I spent a night away from my hotel in order to visit a village mission station, when I returned to the beach I was greeted with anxious cries of "Amma! Amma! Where have you been?" I was quickly surrounded by a sea of concerned traders who had been worried in case I'd fallen sick.

"Now I've told you before, I'm not buying anything from you!" I scolded them playfully. "Oh no, Amma. We only want to talk to you!" they replied, quite hurt that I suspected them of mercenary motives!

I became very fond of one young man called Shibu who was a waiter in one of the small restaurants. He told me that his 'bed' was actually one of the restaurant tables! At night, after clearing up he would settle down to sleep on one of these hard tables. He wasn't complaining, simply stating a fact. As for bathroom facilities, he merely shrugged when I asked him. He was worried about his father, a poor farmer, as there had been a serious shortage of rain in Kerala due to several poor monsoon seasons. He said: "Please Madam, ask your Jesus to send rain." I said a quick prayer with him, asking the Lord to send lots of rain that year and thought no more about it. Imagine my surprise when, some months later I received an anxious email from Shibu asking me if I was still praying for rain, and if so would I please stop as the roads were flooded and bridges had been washed away in the downpour!

On another occasion whilst in Gujarat, a priest showed me his garden with its badly parched soil. As the rains had been poor he couldn't spare water for the garden, having to conserve it for drinking. I cheerfully said "Right, I'm going to pray for rain!" Of course he smiled good-naturedly at the eccentric foreign lady but he was nonplussed next morning after a night of unprecedented rain. Normally rain doesn't fall in February! From then on I was known as 'Mrs. Elijah' referring to the prophet Elijah's prayer for rain in the Book of Kings! Our God has a sense of humour.

During my stay at Kovalam Beach, I decided to take a trip to the southernmost tip of India, a fascinating place called Kanyakumari where there is confluence of the Indian Ocean, the Arabian Sea and the Bay of Bengal. From the beach, because of its unique geographical location, you can watch the sun set over the sea in the evening and then enjoy a magnificent sunrise in the morning. My new friend, Shibu, suggested that I hire a car and driver and spend a night in a hotel there and on an impulse I invited Shibu to accompany me. I know my children would have been horrified at the thought of their mother inviting a stranger to join me on such a trip and normally I wouldn't do such a thing, but I was certain that I could trust this gentle young man and my trust was not misplaced.

He turned out to be a delightful travelling companion, stopping the car several times en-route to point out places of interest. A bright and intelligent young man, he had been unable to find work in his home town and in order to support his aged parents had taken the job in the restaurant. This is very common in India, where graduates are often forced to work in shops, restaurants or as taxi drivers. When I asked one young man why this was, he replied "Well, madam, unless you know somebody influential in a company or you have money to pay a bribe, it's very difficult to find a good job." I felt saddened at the waste of talent and wondered how many brilliant minds were not being used because of the bribery and corruption endemic in that culture.

When we reached Kanyakumari, Shibu directed the driver to a good hotel where after dropping me off, he left with the driver, promising to meet me outside in about half an hour. When he returned, he told me that he'd found a place to spend the night. I suspected that this was in fact the back seat of the car, or even out on the beach. After much argument, I finally persuaded Shibu to let me book him into the hotel where I was staying. His eyes filled with tears and

I felt humbled by his gratitude and joy that he was to spend the night in a nice hotel for the first and probably the last time ever. He whispered that he'd never been a guest in a hotel or sat down to order a meal in a restaurant but was always the one who served. He loved everything about the hotel and took great delight in travelling up and down in the lift; I got as much pleasure witnessing Shibu's childlike enjoyment as I did from watching the magnificent sunset and sunrise.

The next day we visited the Church of Our Lady of Ransom which is almost on the beach. Most of the parishioners are poor Tamil fishermen but the church was brightly decorated and the many statues were decked with garlands. As we were leaving, a poor old lady touched me and said something in Tamil. I thought she was begging, but Shibu assured me that she didn't want any money but in fact had blessed me! I felt very honoured and not a little humbled by her graciousness. I was deeply saddened when this whole area was devastated by the terrible tsunami on Boxing Day, 2004 when thousands lost their lives and I couldn't help wondering if that old lady was one of the victims.

After my break at Kovalam Beach I flew up to Mumbai where I spent some time with another of my fellow Dei Verbum students. Hawkinson is a layman who was fortunate enough to be sponsored by his bishop in the Diocese of Bombay with a view to setting up a scripture diploma course. Hawkinson had been a bit of a gangster when he was young but after a powerful conversion experience which had transformed his life he had given up his shady business interests and dedicated his life to serving the Lord. After his return from Nemi he had set up a small Bible Academy in a local Catholic High School. He invited me to stay with his family in their house overlooking the Arabian Sea. As the temperature and humidity were rising daily, I was delighted that my bed was in a covered in verandah which enjoyed a refreshing ocean breeze. I enjoyed my early morning tea looking out over the colourful garden, watching hordes of chattering monkeys swinging through the trees!

The Bible Academy is a rather grand name for what is in fact a couple of shabby classrooms in a run-down school. When I gave a talk there one evening I was touched by the level of enthusiasm and desire to learn scripture; their eagerness was in sharp contrast to the indifference we see in our affluent parishes in the west. One mention of 'bible study' is enough to send most parishioners scurrying out of the door posthaste! Despite the Dickensian conditions, these men and women had willingly travelled across the city after a hard day's work in order to sit in a dusty classroom to study the bible. I could only admire the dedication of Hawkinson and his assistants as they determinedly over-looked the lack of facilities and the marauding rats, in order to offer scripture courses to these poor people who were so desperate to learn more about the bible.

I was often invited to give talks in schools and I was struck by the level of interest and enthusiasm of the students. In complete contrast to many of our bored or indifferent teenagers, the young people in India were invariably curious and very interested to hear about life in the west and their lack of sophistication was refreshing. How to describe snow to somebody who has only ever seen a picture of it? I was asked "what does it feel like" and "what's it like to walk through?" One young man said: "Does it hurt you when it's falling?" I was also struck by the respectfulness of children in India where it is unacceptable to be rude to an adult. Wherever I went, I was invariably followed by groups of smiling children chanting: "Hello Aunty! What is your good name please?"

I have been to India five times now; travelling extensively from the Himalayas in the north down to Kanyakumari the southernmost tip and I found that unlike our secular society, people are generally more spiritually open and receptive to the gospel. However, in some states due to an upsurge of Hindu fundamentalism, there is a growing hostility to Christianity and it is forbidden to preach the gospel anywhere other than in a Christian Church. Converts from Hinduism have been severely beaten and in the case of women, some have been covered in tar and had their beautiful long hair hacked off.

In most regions of India the Catholic Schools I visited were places where children and staff of various faiths worked happily side by side and only in those areas where political agitators stir up anti-Christian feelings is there trouble. I visited the convent of Sister Rani Maria in Madhya Pradesh, one of the states where there has been an upsurge of violence and bigotry. Sister Rani Maria had been active in helping the poor to defend their rights against unscrupulous landowners who tried to defraud them of their land. These landowners are powerful men who are often in league with the local police and politicians, paying them handsome bribes to turn a blind eye to their cruelty and injustice to the poor. Despite threats made against her, Sister Rani Maria stood firm in her resolve to help the poor achieve justice.

One morning she set out early to travel to an outlying village where she was to address a group of field labourers. After some time, the bus she was travelling on came to a sudden halt in a remote area and Sister Rani Maria was ordered off the bus by several fellow passengers. In front of the other passengers, Sister Rani Maria was viciously beaten and stabbed to death by one of these men and her body was cruelly dumped at the roadside. Not one person lifted a finger to help her. It turned out that the killer was a desperately poor and uneducated young man who had been paid a large sum of money by local landowners to kill the courageous little nun.

There was such a public outcry in the local community that the authorities could no longer ignore the murder and a neighbouring police force was enlisted to track down the killer. Sister Rani Maria's family went to visit the man in jail and just as Pope John Paul II had forgiven his attacker; this humble family forgave their sister's murderer. As a result of this, there was reconciliation between the local Catholics and their Hindu neighbours just as Rani Maria would have wanted and in this way at least some good came from her death.

Certain states are very dangerous and priests have been unjustly accused of the most heinous crimes in an effort to discredit Christianity in general and the Catholic Church in particular. Sadly in recent years there has been an upsurge of violence against Christians and the Catholic Church throughout India. This has been orchestrated by powerful politicians who wish to maintain the status quo and resent the role the church has plays in campaigning for civil rights and justice for the poor. Many priests have been murdered and nuns brutally raped whilst the authorities turned a blind eye. But the vast majority of people in India just want to live side by side with their neighbours in peace and harmony and it is a small but vociferous minority who stir up hatred for political gain.

In general Indians are very spiritual and in the schools I visited and spoke in, the children asked me a lot of questions about religious practices in the west. When I explained that many people don't believe in God they were astonished. The concept of atheism was alien to them and they couldn't understand how people could live without any form of religious belief. Each home usually has a niche for their favourite idol and daily offerings are made in the hope that this particular deity will protect them or increase their wealth.

When I told the schoolchildren that my country was largely unbelieving, they asked me: "Well who do your people think created the world?" They were obviously puzzled at the thought of a universe which accidentally came into being. In a country where businessmen on their way to work, housewives out shopping and children en-route for school routinely stop at local temples to offer puja (a devotional offering) to their favourite deities, atheism was a difficult concept to explain. When people make their offering of sweets, flowers or coconut to the idol, the priest tending the shrine puts a dot of sandalwood paste on their forehead as a mark of their homage and in return he expects to receive money. This is a perfectly acceptable practice throughout India where most businesses would not dream of starting the day without making an offering to their favourite god. In southern India particularly, syncretism is very common and pictures of various Hindu gods sit alongside pictures of Jesus and Mary!

I was often invited to visit temples by my hosts but as I refused to offer puja to the idols, it became easier to just tell people that I'd rather not go to any more temples! I was saddened to see large numbers of westerners eagerly buying puja offerings of sweets and flowers before joining long queues to bow low before a garish idol.

I was especially horrified at the shrine to Kali the goddess of destruction, situated close to Mother Teresa's Home for the Dying in Calcutta. Shoes have to be removed before one can enter a temple and at this particular one, dozens of goats are slaughtered in full view of the public each day and offered to the idol. Western tourists eagerly joined the crowds as they walked barefoot through the temple, the ground sticky with the blood of countless goats. Upon reaching the idol they bowed low and humbly made an offering of sweets or a garland of flowers. I was both sickened and saddened by the sight. Had Christianity really failed these people so badly that they had to seek after foreign gods? I quickly left and vowed never to set foot in another temple.

I had an interesting encounter outside a Catholic Church in

Varanasi, also known as Benares; sited on the Ganges, it is one of Hinduism's most sacred cities. After looking at the art work in the hot, dusty church I sought shade beneath one of the many tamarind trees in the gardens. Nearby a young man was singing a modern praise song and I quietly finished off the verse for him, as he'd obviously forgotten the words; he smiled and asked if he might join me. As he sat down, a scripture verse came to mind and I felt prompted to share it with him. Tears sprang to his eyes as he told me that not long before I came along, he'd been praying and asking the Lord to give him a sign that the course of action he was planning to take was the right one. Apparently the verse I'd shared was very significant for him and he took this as a sign from the Lord!

Once again I saw how the Lord's great love crosses cultural and religious divides. This young man belonged to a small Pentecostal church and he was obviously surprised at how the Lord had used a foreign lady to answer his prayer and a Catholic at that! He was surprised to learn that I am reasonably familiar with scripture and it is obvious that the suspicion with which Catholics are regarded is widespread and I hoped that our conversation had gone some way towards dispelling some of the myths he'd heard. As I took my leave once more of this incredible country, I promised that God willing, I would return again.

CHAPTER TWENTY-THREE

Yesterday, Today, and Forever

Silver or gold I do not have,
but what I have I give you
(Acts 3:6)

Having missed the worst of the winter weather at home it was a joy to be invited back to Poland in springtime and this time I would be teaching English.   My friend Father Andrew, having returned from Papua New Guinea to take up PhD studies in Poland is the director of a language school run by the Divine Word Missionaries. They offer reasonably priced courses in several languages in contrast to other language schools which are run for profit and are quite expensive.   The school is situated in Nysa, a small town in Silesia close to the Czech Republic. Although not officially trained to teach English as a second language, I seem to have an aptitude for it and as the students I taught were intermediate or advanced level, my lack of Polish was not too much of a handicap!

I bought myself a second hand bicycle to get around on and I enjoyed the warmth of both the people and the weather! At weekends I often gave my testimony through an interpreter in local churches and people would ask me to pray with them, especially for problems with alcohol addiction as there is quite a high incidence of alcoholism in Poland. It is exciting to see the Lord at work despite language barriers and cultural differences. He truly is the same Lord, yesterday today and forever!

During my free time I enjoyed exploring the area on my bicycle and one day whilst cycling through the local park I saw two men approaching who were obviously the worse for drink. I just knew they would stop me and my heart sank.

"Oh no Lord," I grumbled as they stumbled towards me; "Why me?" I was not afraid as I was sure they meant me no harm but simply wanted money, no doubt to buy more drink. However, they were out of luck as far as that was concerned but I had something better than money to give them.

As I was out cycling I hadn't taken any money with me and I tried to explain this to them but of course they didn't speak English. Then I had a sudden inspiration, remembering the words of Peter when he addressed the lame beggar outside of the Beautiful Gate (Acts 3:6). I looked them straight in the eye, laid a hand upon each of their heads and taking a deep breath I said: "I have neither silver nor gold, but what I have I give you in the name of Jesus Christ." I asked the Lord to bless them, give them peace and release them from whatever bound them.

I don't know exactly what happened to them, but the Lord obviously touched them because they both became very emotional and tears coursed down their grubby cheeks. They shook my hand over and over and thanked me profusely before continuing happily, if a little unsteadily on their way! They certainly got more than they bargained for when they stopped me! As I rode back to the house, I had an overwhelming sense of the Lord's love for these two poor men who had fallen on hard times. Only the Lord knew the difficulties in their lives which had led them to this sorry state. And after all, who was I to judge them? I could not help but think; there but for the grace of God go I.

On another occasion I was returning to Nysa on the bus after spending the day in Wroclaw, when I got into conversation with a young student who was going home for the weekend. As she was keen to practice her English on a native speaker, I invited her to visit me at the SVD house. When she arrived, I immediately had a word of knowledge about something bad which had happened to her years ago. But how could I broach this? This can be tricky as you can't just blurt out sensitive matters which might hurt or embarrass people, but I was sure that if the Lord had allowed me this insight it was because He wanted to heal this girl in some way.

After we'd chatted and had a cup of tea, I showed her around the complex and we finally visited the chapel. As we sat there I asked her a leading question and she burst into tears. After she'd composed herself she admitted that this nasty incident had happened when she was young and she was shocked that a total stranger could have such knowledge. I explained to her about the gift of the word of knowledge that the Holy Spirit sometimes gives us and told her that it's because Jesus loves her so much that he wanted to heal her. She was amazed, as like many Catholics she had never heard of such a thing, any more than I had until I came into Renewal. After a short time of prayer, with her permission of course, I asked Jesus to heal this painful memory. She said that she was willing to forgive the person who had harmed her, but as forgiveness is a process, she knew that it would take time and could only be accomplished by the grace of God. The main thing was that she was at least willing to forgive and she left looking and feeling much happier. We have kept in touch with each other and she even visited my home one summer.

Like this young woman, there were many hurtful incidents in my past which had prevented me from receiving God's love. I grew up believing that I had to keep a set of laws, go to Mass every Sunday and be 'good' in order to please God. I didn't realise that I could never earn or deserve God's love and religion for me was little more than trying to keep a set of rules and regulations in order to appease a demanding God. For most of my life I felt like a hopeless failure because I seemed to lurch from one disaster to another. Some of the problems were of my own making of course, but even when we make a mess of our lives God can restore things and put them right.

Recently whilst in Brighton attending a healing conference, I reflected on how my life had changed since the days when I'd worked there and how different my life is now. When I was young I lived a life of utter futility, drifting from one dead end relationship to another, drunk for much of the time and heading for disaster.

With the gentle sound of the waves lifting the shingle and the plaintive cry of a seagull for company, I strolled along Brighton seafront remembering those days in the 'Swinging Sixties' when I worked in a large hotel and lived for the weekends when the Mods and Rockers roared into town. I spent most of my free time going from pub to pub seeking excitement but one night I narrowly escaped getting into serious trouble. Some of my fellow workers at the hotel had tried to persuade me to join them on a night out but for some reason I didn't feel comfortable about going out with them and politely declined their offer.

"Come on," they said, "Don't be a stick in the mud! It'll be a good laugh". As I was at a loose end that night, I was tempted to join them but thankfully something prevented me from joining them. How glad I was that for once I followed my instincts because I never saw any of those people again. They were arrested for armed robbery, including an unsuspecting girl who had gone along instead of me! One of the men had a gun and they had decided to rob a filling station and wanted a girl to go with them to act as a decoy. When I refused, they persuaded another naïve girl who thought she was going for a night out and instead became embroiled in a serious crime. I was shocked when I realised it could so easily have been me standing trial. I believe now that God was protecting me, despite my ungodly lifestyle which is another good reason for me not to be too ready to judge and condemn others.

Walking in the cool night air along Brighton seafront, a place that once held so many bad memories, I thanked God for giving me a second chance when I had made such a mess of my life. I feel that God healed those memories and I can now visit Brighton without any sense of regret. God has taken away my feelings of shame and transformed them into thankfulness for his mercy.

For much of my life I despised myself and envied those who had led 'good' lives. Although I regret having hurt people in the past, I cannot undo what I did, only try to live a better life now. Although I have by no means arrived, at least I'm enjoying the journey. I am thankful that I have a loving family and many good friends. My daughter Helen, who was brought back into our lives in such a wonderful way, is proving to be a very special member of the family. There is no doubt in my mind that God's timing is perfect and I'm grateful that Helen and Warren at least had a chance to meet before he died.

Speaking of gratitude, I don't know about other people but I often find myself praying for somebody's needs after they send out a desperate plea. However, it's not very often that people will bother to let you know the outcome and one day after praying for a particularly desperate situation, I was waiting to hear what happened. Finally I could wait no longer and I rang the person who had been so desperate for prayer. "Oh, everything worked out fine" she said breezily. "Well, thanks for letting me know!" I said to myself, some-what miffed that she had not even bothered to let me know after I'd spent hours trying to help and praying about the situation. Immediately the thought occurred to me: "Who are you to complain? How do you think God feels?" Rather sheepishly I had to admit that many times I fail to thank God for a good outcome when I've prayed desperately for him to help me and I was reminded of the story Jesus told of the ten lepers who were healed when only one of them bothered to return and thank him (Luke 17:12-19).

My walk with the Lord since that night in February 1985 continues to be exciting, if not always easy. The Lord didn't actually promise us an easy life or guarantee prosperity as some over enthusiastic T.V. evangelists would have us believe. In fact Jesus warns us: "In the world you will have tribulation." You might say this is the bad news! But this is immediately followed by the good news! "But be of good cheer, for I have overcome the world" (John 16:33).

Whilst trying to follow Christ is not an easy option, neither is it dull and Christianity has been poorly served by those who misrepresent the Good News with a narrow legalistic interpretation, giving the false impression that it is boring and restrictive.

Yes, Jesus said: "It is a narrow gate and a hard road that leads to life, and only a few find it" (Matt 7:13-14), but that doesn't mean narrow-mindedness. Jesus didn't come to bind us with a set of rules and rituals but to set us free to love God in order that we might have a relationship with a loving Father. He came that we might have life and have it in abundance (John 10:10).

As I reflect upon my life and the many wrong paths I took before the Lord brought me back on track, I realise that just

like the father in the story of the Prodigal Son, our Heavenly
Father waits patiently for us and never gives up on us even
when we are far from Him, and He just longs for us to be
reconciled to Him. In this wonderful story that Jesus tells of
the man and his two sons (Luke 15:11-32), we hear that:
"While he was still a long way off, his father saw him and
was moved with pity." Worldly wisdom would tell us that
the father ought to have made sure the son was sorry
for what he'd done before he forgave him. And as for
showering him with gifts and throwing a party, well that's
just plain crazy! No wonder his brother was so miffed! But
God's ways are not our ways (Is. 55:8), and just like the
father in this story, He loves us with an extravagant love
and is just waiting for an opportunity to restore us.
Perhaps just like that Prodigal Son, many of us have to
travel the way of darkness in order to appreciate the light
when at last we find it? I believe that I did.

Once when I was talking to a priest about the mess I had
made of my life, I told him how I regretted the stupid
mistakes I'd made. I had lurched from one crisis to another
– many of them of my own making. "Oh no Margaret," he
said, "don't regret your life because that's what makes you
the person you are today and God has used those mistakes
to shape you and encourage others." It certainly helped me
to look more positively at my life and see how indeed God
can turn our disasters into blessings. Romans 8:28 says:
"We know that by turning everything to their good, God
co-operates with all those who love Him, with all those that
He has called according to his purpose."

I believe without a shadow of a doubt that God does have a

purpose for each of our lives and loves us unconditionally, whether we acknowledge Him or not. I also believe He has a sense of humour and delights in His children, just as I delight in the antics of my grand-children. I agree with the Victorian poet, George McDonald, who said:

> *"It is the heart that is not yet sure of its God that is afraid to laugh in His presence."*

I have enough confidence now in God's love for me to be able to laugh at myself at times and not take myself too seriously. When I am tempted to pride, a moment's reflection on the willingness of Jesus, the Lord of Lords and King of Kings, to empty Himself and become a humble carpenter soon dispels that! The thought of Jesus kneeling with a towel around His waist, in the manner of a servant, washing the feet of humble fishermen, is enough to show us how ridiculous we are at times with our spiritual posturing and self-importance. One look in the mirror soon reminds me of who I really am and what I would be without Jesus at the centre of my life.

I would encourage anybody who may be feeling that their circumstances are hopeless or that they've wandered too far from God, not to give up hope and to believe that the moment we turn to God, he will help us in our weakness. He's just waiting for the opportunity. As I write these words, the relentless rain has finally stopped and I thought: "Ah, thank goodness the sun is back!" It suddenly dawned on me that in fact, the sun had never gone away it was simply obscured by the clouds. And I believe it's the same with God; He's always there although often His presence is obscured because of the circumstances of our lives or our own sinfulness. God is always looking for an opportunity to bless us and the moment we turn to Him, the 'clouds roll away' and He will be there for us.

When Warren died, I felt that I'd hit rock bottom and now looking back I can say; yes, I've been to the bottom and the bottom is solid because Jesus is my rock and He was there for me. His promises can be trusted.

I know that many parents despair of their children and worry about those who may have turned away from their faith and again I would say, don't give up on them – God hasn't! I believe with all of my heart that none of our prayers go unheard and in my own case, although only one of my children currently practices their faith, I am trusting and believing that God will hear and answer my prayers for them and that even if it's after I have left this earth, they will come to know and love Jesus.

I don't know what the future holds for me but I pray that I continue to live with a sense of anticipation and hope. I have just embarked on another degree course. Despite my initial scepticism about studying theology, I decided to do a post graduate course in Practical Theology which will keep me busy for the next couple of years. And next year I plan to complete the second part of a counselling course at the University. In addition, there are many more places I would like to visit and as I have outstanding invitations from missionary friends in the Philippines and Indonesia, who knows what further adventures lie ahead?

If I am tempted to anxiety I remind myself of God's promise in Jeremiah 29:11-13

> *"I know the plans I have in mind for you says the Lord,*
> *plans for peace and not disaster, reserving a future*
> *full of hope for you. When you call on me,*
> *when you pray to me I shall answer.*
> *When you seek me with all of your heart*
> *you shall find me".*

These are my words of life, my words of hope and my promise from God that He does have a purpose for me which He will reveal as I walk with him into the future, one day at a time. I have at last accepted who I am. I can put away the masks, look in the mirror and know that I am loved and cherished by God who sent His Son to light up my darkness and set me free to be me!

Further copies of this book
are available from

Goodnews Books & Resources
St. John the Apostle Church Buildings
296 Sundon Park Road
Luton, Beds. LU3 3AL, UK

+44 01582 571011
orders@goodnewsbooks.net
www.goodnewsbooks.net